Hendon parish church, by J.S. Whitty, 1868

HENDON

CHILD'S HILL, GOLDERS GREEN AND MILL HILL

A Pictorial History

The arms of the borough of Hendon, 1932-65. Prepared by the College of Arms, the design combines various local references. The shield, for instance, shows the lamb and the flag, originally from St Mary's church weathervane and used as an emblem by Hendon Local Board and Urban District Council from 1879-1932. The lamb stands on a hill for Childs Hill under two windmill sails for Mill Hill. The crest is a winged propellor commemorating the aerodrome.

HENDON

CHILD'S HILL, GOLDERS GREEN AND MILL HILL

A Pictorial History

Stewart Gillies and Pamela Taylor

Barnet Libraries Arts and Museums

Phillimore

1993

Published by
PHILLIMORE & CO. LTD.
Shopwyke Manor Barn, Chichester, Sussex

ISBN 0 85033 875 1

Printed and bound in Great Britain by
BIDDLES LTD.
Guildford, Surrey

List of Illustrations

Frontispiece: Borough of Hendon Coat of
Arms, 1932-65

1. Hendon section of the O.S. map, 1822
2. Roman moulded-face flagon neck from
   Church Terrace
3. St Mary's Hendon, 1807
4. Norman font at St Mary's Hendon
5. Entry for Hendon in Domesday Book
6a. Beating the Bounds broadside, 1865
6b. Beating the Bounds at Finchley Lane
   bridge, 1926
7. Brent Bridge on the Edgware Road, 1799
8. The River Brent at Finchley Lane and
   Waverley Grove, *c.*1900
9. Hendon Place, 1780
10. Ashley Lane, *c.*1898
11. Hendon House, 1796
12. Copthall, 1908
13. Nicoll Almshouses, *c.*1893
14. Church End, *c.*1896
15. Daniel's Almshouses and Bennet's school,
   1888
16. Highwood House, 1817
17. *The Three Crowns* in the 1880s
18. Colindeep Lane in the early 20th century
19. Bell Lane, 1883
20. Rosebank, 1976
21. Moat Mount in the early 20th century
22. Hendon Hall in the early 20th century
23. Golders Green, 1789
24. Woodstock House sale catalogue, 1888
25. *The White Swan* in the early 20th century
26. The happy shepherd with a view of Child's
   Hill, 1784
27. Mill Hill School, 1807
28. Mill Hill Congregational chapel, *c.*1860
29. James Murray and schoolmasters at Mill
   Hill School in the 1870s
30. Hendon Poor Law Union workhouse in
   the early 20th century
31. Goodyers, *c.*1927
32. Albert Cottage, 1912
33. Rural sports broadside, 1801
34. *The Plough* in the 1880s
35. Mrs. Cole, 1882

36. Vine Cottage, 1958
37. Finchley Road, *c.*1906
38. Temple Fortune in the early 20th century
39a. Theodore Williams
39b. St Paul's Mill Hill, *c.*1904
40. Hendon Vicarage, 1904
41. Parish pump at Brent Street, 1828
42. Brent Green, *c.*1850
43. Belmont Farm, Mill Hill in the 1880s
44. Woodfield House, *c.*1940
45. Our Lady of Dolours in the 1900s
46. All Saints' Child's Hill in the early 20th
   century
47. Hendon station in the early 20th century
48. The Halt at The Hale, 1906
49. St Joseph's College prior to the mid-1930s
50. St Vincent's, *c.*1932
51. Hendon section of the O.S. map, 1896
52. *The Rose and Crown, c.*1872
53. Brent Street in the early 20th century
54. Gothic Cottage in the early 19th century
55. Colonel Bacon and family at Tudor
   House, 1902
56. St Swithin's, *c.*1900
57. Sunningfields Crescent, 1901
58. The Dowding family at Brook Lodge in
   the 1890s
59a. Sunningfields Lawn Tennis Club in the
   1890s
59b. Hendon Athletic Sports Club in the 1890s
60. Hendon and Cricklewood Rifle Club, 1906
61a. Burroughs Lodge, 1901
61b. The lake at Burroughs Lodge, 1901
62. The Burroughs pond in the early 20th
   century
63. The Burroughs in the 1890s
64. Welsh Harp poster, 19th century
65a. The London Swimming Club's festival at
   the Welsh Harp, 1870
65b. Wrestling at the Welsh Harp, *c.*1870
66. Schweppe's advertisement, *c.*1900
67. The *Cricklewood Tavern, c.*1915
68. St Peter's Cricklewood, *c.*1905

69. St Saviour's Homes, Brent Street, 1897
70. Brampton Grove, c.1930
71. Butchers Lane, 1895
72. Edgware Road, 1903
73a. Goldbeaters Farm, 1887
73b. Goldbeaters Farm dining room, 1927
74. Central London Sick Asylum, Colindale, 1899
75. Mill Hill village in the early 20th century
76. The Ridgeway and Boltons Stores in the early 20th century
77. Laying the foundation stone of Hendon Town Hall, 1900
78. Hendon Volunteer Fire Brigade, c.1880
79. U.D.C. election handbill, 1902
80. Golders Hill Terrace, 1904
81. The tea terrace at Golders Hill Park, 1915
82. Coronation celebrations in Sunny Hill Fields, 1902
83. Hoop Lane, Golders Green, c.1915
84. Dollis Farm, Holders Hill Road, pre-1930
85. Bittacy Farm, c.1902
86. A military funeral at Mill Hill in the early 20th century
87. The Avenue, Cricklewood, c.1905
88. Cook's Corner and Church Road in the early 20th century
89. Vine Cottages, Greyhound Hill, 1912
90. Salisbury Plain, 1912
91. *The Green Man*, The Hale, c.1908
92. Cricklewood Broadway, c.1912
93. *The Castle* inn, Childs Hill, c.1906
94. Wyldes Farm, c.1909
95. Golders Green crossroads, 1906
96. The Promenade, Golders Green, in the early 20th century
97. Golders Green Hippodrome, 1932
98. Willifield Way, c.1915
99. Hampstead Garden Suburb club house, 1916
100. Spalding Hall, Victoria Road, 1914-18
101. Highfield, Golders Green Road, in the 1920s
102. Melvin Hall, Golders Green Road, 1932
103. Hendon Cottage Hospital, c.1927
104. Manor House Hospital in the 1920s
105. The dining room at Ivy House, probably in the 1920s
106. West Hendon Broadway, c.1914
107. Claude Grahame-White, 1910
108. Hendon Aerodrome programme, 1912
109. Greyhound Hill, c.1912
110. Employees leaving the Airco factory, Edgware Road, c.1917
111. Car production at Grahame-White's factory in the early 1920s
112. The Victory Aerial Derby, 1919
113. The Hyde in the early 20th century
114. Unveiling of the Hendon War Memorial, 1922
115. The Silk Stream at the Welsh Harp, 1922
116. Mill Hill Broadway, c.1930
117. Mill Hill Garden Estate sale catalogue, 1920s
118. Lilley Lane in the early 1920s
119. Elliott Road in the early 1920s
120. Hendon Central station, 1923
121. Hendon Central Circus and Watford Way, 1928
122. A Burroughs Farm dairy cart, pre-1920
123a. Brent Street, c.1920
123b. Bell Lane, c.1925
124. Cricklewood Lane in the 1920s
125. Goldbeaters Grove, c.1930
126. Woodcroft Hall, Watling Avenue, c.1930
127. Watling Avenue, 1948
128. Clitterhouse Farm, 1926
129. The Golders Green Estate, Clitterhouse, in the 1930s
130. Fiveways Corner, 1927
131. Hendon Way near The Vale, 1935
132. Apex Corner in the 1940s
133. Golders Green Road, 1927
134. Widening the Bell Lane bridge, 1931
135. Brent Cross, c.1947
136. The Splash, Hale Lane, c.1925
137. The Home Seekers Guide to Mill Hill, c.1925
138. Dole Street in the early 20th century
139. The forge, Holcombe Hill, c.1935
140. The Burroughs, c.1930
141. Hendon sewage works, 1930
142. Hendon Library, 1930s
143. Grove House, The Burroughs, 1933
144. Mill Hill Fire Station, 1929
145. West Hendon pool, 1925
146. The Regal cinema, 1932
147. The Ambassador cinema, 1932
148. Church Road from The Quadrant, 1952
149. The dining room, *Brent Bridge Hotel*, c.1935
150. A telescope at the London University Observatory, Mill Hill
151. The Hendon synagogue, Raleigh Close, 1939
152. West Heath Court, c.1936
153. Staples Corner, c.1937
154. Duple coachworks brochure, 1936
155. Hendon Charter Day celebrations, 1932
156. Hendon Technical Institute, The Burroughs, 1939
157. 'Rout the Rumour' rally, 1940
158. Royal visit to bomb damage at Colindale

159. The Victoria British Restaurant, Brent Street, 1943
160. Bomb damage at West Hendon, 1941
161. The National Institute for Medical Research, Mill Hill, 1950
162. The opening of Church Farm House Museum, 1955
163. Church End Farm, 1939
164a. North Street and New Brent Street, 1958
164b. Granville Road, 1962
165. Colindale Trolleybus Depot, c.1960
166. M1 roadworks, Station Road, Mill Hill, 1965

Acknowledgements

The Archives & Local Studies Centre has so rich a collection of Hendon material thanks to the activities over many years of a number of dedicated people. Amongst these we should like to acknowledge especially Norman Brett-James, Ralph Calder, A. G. Clark, John Collier, Andrew Forsyth, Brigid Grafton Green, Frances Gravatt, Hendon Library staff, Nicky Hillman, Fred Hitchin-Kemp, Christopher Ikin, John Maltby, Dave Ruddom, Ted Sammes and David Sullivan.

The collection has also benefited greatly from the research activities of members of the Hendon and District Archaeological Society (HADAS) and the Mill Hill and Hendon Historical Society. Both have published works on various subjects, and the latter has transferred its rich collection of sources and unpublished files to the Centre.

There are other books to which users and curators of the collection turn constantly, particularly Alan A. Jackson, *Semi-Detached London* (1973; second edition 1991), M. Miller and A. S. Gray, *Hampstead Garden Suburb* (1992), and the Hendon chapter in the *Victoria County History of Middlesex*, Volume V (1976).

Both the size of the area and the wealth of material have made omissions unavoidable. We have tried to be relatively more generous to less well known areas and aspects, and avoid duplicating much that is readily available in other publications. Some omissions, however, as well as the inevitable mistakes, will reflect gaps in our knowledge. Anyone who can help by remedying gaps of any sort will aid the ever-continuing improvement of the collection for future users.

Illustration Acknowledgements

The authors wish to thank the following for the use of illustrations: Andrew Forsyth, 53, 62, 88, 123a, 135, 146; Margaret Heather, 122; Nicky Hillman, 96, 97; John Laing Limited, 129; Ted Sammes, 2; D. A. Thompson, 165. The rest of the illustrations come from the collections of Barnet Libraries' Archives & Local Studies Centre.

Introduction

The ancient manor and parish of Hendon covered a large area of well over 8,000 acres and numerous settlements. The name, which means 'at the high down', refers to today's Church End, whose site on the top of Greyhound Hill clearly explains the description. According to recent research, Hendon is also a particularly interesting place-name because it may well come from the first period of Anglo-Saxon settlement (mid-fifth century to before 800), and could show the incomers' awareness of a pre-existing settlement. This would be supported by the finds from an excavation at Church End in 1973-4, which included various Roman remains of the late third to early fourth century.

Church End may have given the name Hendon to the whole district, but it was probably never the only settlement. There have been a few other Roman and earlier finds, including a late third- or early fourth-century rubbish pit at Burnt Oak, well away from the high plateau. There were at least two Roman roads running northwards through the area, both of which may well have followed earlier routes. Part of one lies under Copthall Fields. The other, the Edgware Road (Watling Street) which forms most of Hendon's western boundary, was the main Roman road from London to St Albans and the north. On it at Brockley Hill, just north of Hendon, was Sullionacis, a large pottery-making centre. The potters, though, seem to have been itinerant, as had been many earlier 'residents'. The revolutionary shift to settled farming did not occur until the New Stone Age (Neolithic), from about 3500BC, and many local finds are earlier than this. The important encampment at West Heath, straddling the Hendon-Hampstead border, which has yielded over 100,000 flints, was about 4,000 years earlier.

Hendon was always an area of small scattered settlements, not simply because of its size, but also because most of its soil is heavy clay. This leads to woods, clearings mainly for pasture, and small hamlets, rather than the large open fields and villages of the more fertile corn-growing areas. Right up to the 19th century local settlers normally chose hilltop sites, which had the best drainage and sometimes a covering of lighter soil. By the mid-10th century there were various districts centred on separate settlements. The name of Hendon was applied only to what is now the central belt north of the Brent. North of this was Lothersley, which centred somewhere along the Mill Hill Ridgeway. The small area west of the Edgware Road, which today still forms a distinctive outcrop on the borough's map, was in 957 part of Tunworth, modern Kingsbury, but soon afterwards came with Lothersley to Westminster Abbey. It is through the abbey's deeds that we know these names and transfers, but unfortunately many of these deeds were reworked in the 12th century, making it hard to separate facts from the monks' later fictions. The monks certainly believed that Blechenham, which covered most of the area south of the Brent and may have centred on the hill at Temple Fortune, had been granted to them by King Offa of Essex, who ruled in the early eighth century. It definitely belonged to them in the mid-10th, as did Codenhleawe, which probably centred on Child's Hill, and whose name may have survived in Cowhouse.

By the end of the 10th century, then, Hendon had probably assumed more or less its later shape, united as one estate, or manor, belonging to the abbey of Westminster. It appears as such in Domesday Book, written in 1086. This is the first of a number of medieval surveys which allow us to see a surprising amount about the life and development of the area. In 1086 most of the manor was still covered in dense woodland – estimated as enough to support 1,000 pigs. The population was small, probably under 300, but since Domesday only writes about the manor as a whole we do not know how many settlements there were. As clearing progressed the number of settlements, and interconnecting paths, probably increased, but the earliest references may well occur long after a place first existed. Frith (which means wooded country), Cricklewood, The Hale, Hodford, The Hyde (all also Anglo-Saxon words) were all there by the 13th century, and The Burroughs and Highwood Hill by the fourteenth. Mill Hill is first recorded in 1374, the name reflecting the manor mill on what is now Mill Field. The mill itself vanished in the 18th century.

Wood and pasture were always important, but some arable crops were grown locally in common fields. In 1574 there were four, which were gradually enclosed over time, but there was never a general enclosure and the last strips, in Sheaveshill at Burnt Oak, did not succumb until the mid-19th century. While Hendon remained a Westminster manor, its economy was also partly integrated with the abbey's other estates: animals were regularly moved between manors, and wood taken to Westminster for building and fuel. Convalescent monks were often sent to benefit from Hendon's better air. The abbot had a house there (though where is unknown) by 1285, but a new one was finished in Parson Street in 1326. This remained the manor house when Hendon passed into lay hands in 1551 after the Dissolution of the Monasteries and suppression of the short-lived Bishopric of Westminster. The house (which played host to many famous visitors) was known as Hendon Place (later Tenterden Hall), and was frequently altered and rebuilt until its demolition in 1936.

Because the manor of Hendon was unified and strong it kept its importance well beyond the end of the Middle Ages, and also beyond the sale of all the manorial demesne lands. Enclosure of the 'waste' or uncultivated land was an important issue in the 18th and 19th centuries, when there was pressure to build on the wide roadside verges. This was particularly important because Hendon, unlike most of its neighbours, lacked any large common. By 1890 E. Evans, the local historian, reported that 'The waste of the manor seems to have been granted away wholesale, till there is now hardly a rood of common land in the parish; so that there is nothing to prevent the whole area being covered with bricks and mortar'. There is even today a lord of the manor, but the manorial organisation was wound up with the last manor court, held (like many of its predecessors) at the *White Bear* in 1916.

In the late 16th century the weakness of many manors, and the general shake-up after the Dissolution, led Queen Elizabeth to transfer responsibility for most local government from the manor to the parish. In Hendon the parish had been based on the manor and therefore covered the same area. The earliest references to the church, St Mary's at Church End, and the earliest surviving parts of its fabric both date to the 12th century, but there was a priest at Hendon in 1086 who may have used some less permanent structure. Even before it acquired responsibility for local government the church was very much a focal point for the community, which in a large parish like Hendon meant that many parishioners had a considerable distance to travel. Attendance was not only compulsory but had to be to one's own church, even if the neighbouring parish's was nearer. This was partly to protect each church's income, and the same reason usually prevented the provision of more separate parish churches or even dependent chapels of ease. The first new Anglican chapel (later church) within Hendon was St Paul's Mill Hill, opened despite bitter opposition from Hendon's rector in 1833.

It was during the Elizabethan period that families of wealth and influence began to move into the area; its combination of rural qualities and proximity to London made it a favoured site for country retreats. One of the first of these notable incomers was John Norden, antiquary and mapmaker to Elizabeth I, who lived at Hendon House in Brent Street on a site now occupied by Hendon School. The trend continued into the 17th and 18th centuries – Mill Hill Ridgeway and Highwood Hill with their fine views and pleasant countryside were particularly fashionable. Rachel, Lady Russell had one of her several homes at Highwood House, and resided there occasionally after the execution of her husband, Lord William Russell, for his alleged part in the Rye House Plot (to assassinate Charles II) in 1683.

Other large houses built in Mill Hill at this time included Copt Hall, Littleberries, Holcome House, Hendon Park and Partingdale Manor. Between these mansions many smaller villas and groups of cottages developed including some weatherboarded buildings which still survive. Of these the most notable is Rosebank on The Ridgeway, which was used as a Quaker meeting house in the late 17th century. Nonconformity was certainly strong in Mill Hill. Richard Swift, a minister ejected from Edgware at the Restoration, was jailed a number of times for holding conventicles in his house, Jeanettes, on The Ridgeway, and there were prominent nonconformist families. Celia Fiennes, the diarist and traveller, immortalised as the 'fine lady' in 'Ride a cock horse to Banbury Cross', was one of seven Presbyterians who met at Mary Nicoll's house at Highwood Hill, but as the grand-daughter of Viscount Saye and Sele she was also one of the wealthy incomers, residing at Highwood Ash from 1713 to 1737. Mill Hill's association with nonconformity was revived in 1807 when Mill Hill School was founded as the Protestant Dissenters' Grammar School, to meet the need for a non-Anglican public school. Although lacking the grandeur of Mill Hill, Brent Street was also noted for its fine mansions, and by the 18th century was becoming the biggest hamlet. Its largest residence was the aforementioned Hendon House but there were several others, now all vanished. The gentrification continued further south at Golders Green with a number of ornamental villas appearing from the late 18th century. These were built on enclosures from the roadside manorial waste land.

More modest dwellings and shops clustered around Brent Street's junction with Bell Lane. Cooke's Survey of Hendon of 1796 mentions a wheelwright's shop, a collar-maker's, and a butcher's here, and *The Bell* inn, a venue for rural sports such as pig running, was first recorded in 1751. The hamlet undoubtedly owed some of its prosperity to its position on an important secondary route which formed an alternative to Edgware Road, whose low-lying parts were often flooded. It was also one of the droving routes for meat going into London on the hoof, while local carters transporting Hendon's principle crop, hay, would have used it too, and are commemorated by the surviving (though rebuilt) *Load of Hay* inn.

In 1712 the Edgware Road was put under a turnpike trust to improve it, with a local toll gate on the Hendon-Edgware boundary, just south of the Dean's Brook. However, improvement seems to have been limited for in 1798 Middleton reported in his *View of the Agriculture of Middlesex* that the road had 'mud four inches deep after heavy rain in the summer and nine inches all winter ... the road has been in this condition for many years to the great disgrace of the trustees'.

Flooding and mud were not the only dangers for the coaching traffic. Highwaymen and footpads operated in the area, and it was not until Bow Street Horse Patrols were stationed along the turnpikes after 1805 that this problem was mitigated. Even then isolated incidents continued, especially away from the turnpikes. The heavily wooded stretch of road between Golders Green and Hampstead was particularly prone, with the private carriages of the district's wealthy villa owners providing an especial lure.

Despite the heavy traffic on the Edgware Road there were no major settlements along its Hendon stretch. Cricklewood, which lay partly in Willesden, was a small grouping of farm buildings and the only hamlet between it and the Edgware boundary was The Hyde, also very small and agricultural. The village of Edgware gained more from its position, but a number of coaching inns did appear along the Hendon stretch, including the *Crown* at Cricklewood, the *Old Welsh Harp*, the *George* and the *Red Lion* (on the Kingsbury side) at The Hyde and the *Bald Faced Stag* at Burnt Oak.

Like the hamlets along the road, those at The Hale, Colindeep and Temple Fortune remained small and purely agricultural. Farming activity was influenced by proximity to London, with farmers developing their production to meet the needs of the growing metropolis. From the 16th century until the early 20th century Hendon, like much of northern Middlesex, was given over to growing hay, needed to feed London's huge horse population. Hay-making did not require a large workforce except at harvest time when, from at least the early 19th century, there was a temporary influx of labourers from outside, especially from Ireland. These workers were often housed in barns or in make-shift huts. The Passionist Fathers, operating in the area from the 1840s and established at Woodfield House in the 1850s, provided not only for their spiritual needs, but also for their sustenance with soup kitchens. They also established a wooden chapel in The Burroughs which became the centre of Roman Catholic worship in Hendon until replaced in 1863 by the church of Our Lady of Dolours in Egerton Gardens.

There was very little local industry and it catered largely for the agricultural community with crafts such as blacksmithing and farriery prominent. There was some small-scale brick-making and tile-making, especially at Child's Hill in the early 19th century. At the same time in this area there emerged a hand-laundry industry which largely served the gentry of neighbouring Hampstead. Child's Hill, by then the largest hamlet south of the Brent, had attracted few wealthy residents, but had begun to develop with the arrival of the Finchley Road in 1825.

This new turnpike road was established to improve access to the West End by linking Regents Park with the Great North Road at Tally Ho, North Finchley. It followed an entirely new route from Regents Park to Church End Finchley, entering Hendon at Child's Hill, where a toll gate was erected close to *The Castle* inn, enhancing its importance. At Golders Green the crossroads was created, thus making it a suitable place for (much) later developments and there was another toll at the junction with Weild (later Hoop) Lane. The isolation of Temple Fortune was ended and the *Royal Oak* established to serve the coaching traffic and by the mid-19th century some terraces of cottages had appeared. Nevertheless, 19th-century photographs still record fields and little traffic passing the inns. The Turnpike Trusts were abolished in 1863 and by 1872 all the remaining roads still subject to toll were freed from it. One reason for this, of course, was the decrease in both traffic and tolls as railways captured the long distance traffic.

The railways first arrived in Hendon in 1867. The first was the G.N.R.'s suburban branch line from Finsbury Park, which entered the parish on the impressive viaduct across the Dollis Brook, had a station at Mill Hill (later known as Mill Hill East) and terminated at Edgware. It was a slow and inconvenient route and did not significantly stimulate development. A new station was opened at The Hale in 1906 but, even after suburbanisation in the 1920s, the line did not attract much passenger business. Following the more successful extension of the tube line beyond Golders Green to Edgware in the 1920s, the older line was eventually electrified in 1941 but only as far as Mill Hill East; the continuation to Edgware had already been closed to passengers in 1939, although it was used for goods until 1964. More recently Dollis School has created a nature reserve in the middle of the abandoned track near Copthall.

The second line to come through Hendon was the Midland Railway's main line from Bedford to St Pancras which opened to goods in 1867 and to passengers in 1868 with stations at Bunns Lane (later Mill Hill Broadway), (West) Hendon, and at Child's Hill (later Cricklewood). Once again the service was inconvenient and its impact on development limited. The only exception was at Cricklewood, where massive sidings, goods and coal yards were developed and rows of modest terraces built to house the railway's employees. The sidings were connected by a loop with the London and South Western Railway in 1884, enabling passengers as well as freight to connect with the new line, but Child's Hill never became an important passenger junction and this service ceased in 1902.

The railway also brought crowds of day trippers to the Welsh Harp – the reservoir formed by damming the Brent just below its junction with the Silkstream which was used to maintain the level of the Grand Union Canal. Its leisure potential was enthusiastically exploited by Jack Warner, who with his brother William Perkins Warner held the licence of the *Old* (or *Lower*) *Welsh Harp* inn for 39 years from 1859. They provided a huge range of entertainments, including skating, swimming, boxing and wrestling matches, hunting, shooting and fishing, a concert hall, a menagerie and a skittle saloon. There was even a music hall song about it – 'The Jolliest Place That's Out' – sung by Annie Adams. In 1870 the enormous Bank Holiday crowds persuaded the Midland Railway to open Welsh Harp station. It closed in 1903, as the resort declined in popularity once the area lost its rural attraction. Streets of working-class terraces stretched west from the Edgware Road to the reservoir by the end of the 1890s, a development boosted by the opening of the large Schweppes mineral water factory in 1895.

Elsewhere in Hendon there had been earlier and contrasting developments. By the 1870s the old hamlets were beginning to grow together: Church End, which was now linked to Hendon station by horse omnibus, was joined to Brent Street by Church Road, where housing developed soon after the opening of the railway. Most of the parish, though, remained rural. The very rich were retreating and many of their residences could only survive as private schools, convents and lunatic asylums.

When the grounds of the Hendon Place estate were sold for development in 1862 one of the purchasers was C.F. Hancock, a rich city jeweller, who had earlier bought Hendon Hall to live in. He built several substantial villas in the Parson Street area in the 1870s. Hidden by high walls and plantations and well away from public transport these continued to attract the comfortably off. This was also true of the houses built around Sunny Gardens during the same period. For these wealthy residents in the 1880s and 1890s there was a full social life with garden parties, sports clubs and a range of societies and associations.

A parallel world existed lower down the hill where working-class terraces were developing on either side of Brent Street and Church Lane: by the 1890s Brent Street had become Hendon's main shopping centre. But the picture was not entirely one of prosperity and progress. Many of the major religious sects found it necessary to open soup kitchens and in this they were joined by some of the district's wealthier residents, like Colonel Burgess who opened a soup kitchen at Hendon House.

A Baptist chapel had opened in Brent Street as early as 1832 but, following the opening of Hendon Congregational Church in 1855, it closed in 1857. However, a new one was opened in Finchley Lane in 1878. Both the Baptists and the Congregationalists owed much to local families, the former to the Spaldings of Shire Hall, and the latter to the Smarts, ironmongers of Brent Street, and both produced offshoots at The Hyde and Mill Hill. The Salvation Army also appeared in Brent Street in 1881 in a temporary building and in 1884 General William Booth attended the laying of a foundation stone for a permanent building. For the Anglicans, Christ Church Brent Street opened in 1881 as a chapel of the parish church and the contrasts between the two were soon attracting comment. In 1887 one commentator noted that the vicar preached verbose flowery discourses devoid of doctrine at St Mary's, and telling, practical, simple sermons at Christ Church.

Both the Anglicans and nonconformists had difficulty funding enough school places for the expanding population, but it was Anglican opposition which delayed the establishment of a school board until 1897. There was some cooperation between the two groups. At West Hendon nonconformists contributed to the Anglican school after seeing shoeless children walking the one and half miles to Church End, and in 1889 a School Emergency Committee, composed of members of the Local Board of Health, was established to give grants to schools, regardless of their religious denomination.

Local government throughout Britain gradually altered in the 19th century to take account of changing reality. Hendon's Local Board had been established in 1879, replacing the parish vestry as the agent of local government. It was replaced in 1895 by the U.D.C. (Urban District Council) whose responsibilities included sanitation, drainage, roads, street lighting, the fire service, and bye-law applications. The U.D.C. also superseded the school board under the Education Act of 1902. By 1900 its offices in the old parish workhouse had become inadequate and new purpose-built ones, designed to reflect its elevated status, were opened in The Burroughs in 1901. The building now forms the central portion of the Town Hall for the London Borough of Barnet.

The U.D.C. was immediately faced with the familiar dilemma of providing much needed services without antagonising ratepayers. The Hendon Ratepayers' Protection Committee was a particularly strong lobby, born out of the opposition to the council's Electric Lighting Order, and its members included many prominent residents. However, it was the progressives on the council who eventually won this battle. Hendon's drainage system and roads were praised at an inquiry in 1906 which considered adding Kingsbury to Hendon U.D. This was successfully opposed on the grounds that the inclusion of Kingsbury, notoriously mismanaged and highly rated, would benefit only that parish's landowners. However, the U.D.C.'s efforts to alleviate severe overcrowding in the poorer areas of the parish were somewhat less impressive. In 1903 one councillor described housing in Child's Hill as a 'disgrace to civilisation' but only in 1914 did the U.D.C. feel able to burden its ratepayers with its first housing estate, of 50 houses there.

Despite the expanding population many farms remained, although with hay farming declining with the diminishing use of horsepower, they were turning more to supplying the demand for fresh milk. However, in 1905 Clitterhouse Farm was said to be growing less desirable as a dairy farm since day trippers from London broke down fences, while its building value was steadily rising. This was a harbinger of the changes which came as communication links with London improved.

By 1904 the Metropolitan Electric Tramways had built a tramway along the Edgware Road from Cricklewood to Edgware with eight trams an hour. In 1909 routes between North Finchley and Golders Green and between Golders Green and Hampstead were added and a link between Cricklewood and Child's Hill opened. However, it was the extension of the underground railway that provided the real stimulus to suburban growth.

In 1902 the Underground Electric Company obtained powers to extend to Golders Green its proposed line from Charing Cross to Hampstead and this was linked with another scheme for a surface railway to extend the line across Hendon to Edgware. Houses were under construction before the station opened to passengers in 1907 with local firms like those of Ernest Owers and Farrow and Howkins heavily involved. This was all speculative development: street layout was largely determined by the pattern of land ownership and by the desire to cram in as many houses as possible. There was little thought given to recreation and to open spaces although, fortunately, Golders Hill House and its beautifully landscaped grounds had been acquired by the London County Council (L.C.C.) in 1898 to form Hendon's first public park. The old villas strung out along Golders Green Road began to fall to the suburban advance and by 1908 the first of the smart shopping parades at the centre of Golders Green had opened. Building continued uninterrupted until the outbreak of the First World War, which also postponed the extension of the line to Edgware.

The new houses were immediately successful partly because they were in many ways advanced and strikingly modern. They were fairly highly priced and the area soon became the butt of music hall jokes about petit-bourgeois snobbery.

The underground also gave rise, indirectly, to the development of Hampstead Garden Suburb. The initial plan had been for a station at the old Wyldes farmhouse, but Dame Henrietta Barnett was so horrified at the prospect of housing stretching from her home (Heath End House at Spaniards) across the Wyldes estate that she formed an action committee which bought up a block of land to form the Hampstead Heath Extension. She also planned the transfer of the rest of the estate to a trust in 1906 to become Hampstead Garden Suburb. In contrast to Golders Green, Hampstead Garden Suburb was idealistic in conception and carefully planned. It had its own Act of Parliament enabling its character to be determined by its trustees and their architects, Raymond Unwin and R.B. Parker, with Sir Edwin Lutyens as a consultant. Dame Henrietta's dream was a utopian one where there would be a mix of social classes living in harmony and this led to buildings which ranged from large detached houses overlooking the Heath Extension to small cottages and flats near Temple Fortune. In practice manual workers and artisans were soon forced out by rising prices and rents and the suburb became middle-class. The idealism, though, did attract artists and liberal or even socialist intellectuals. The suburb has always attracted the interest of architectural and social historians and several major studies have been published.

Large-scale change in the north-west of the parish at Colindale came initially not with railways but, unusually, with aeroplanes. Aircraft were first made here by Everett, Edgcumbe and Co. c.1909 and were flown from a field bought by Claude Grahame-White in 1910 to form the nucleus of his London (or Hendon) Aerodrome. Grahame-White's entrepreneurial skills soon transformed it into one of the country's leading airfields and a major centre for the training of pilots. Crowds flocked to see events like the first aerial 'Derby' in 1912 and the first parachute drop in 1914. There were displays and exhibitions including dangerous stunts such as looping the loop and illuminated night flying. In time the visitors were provided with a club-house, a 30-bedroomed hotel, and five viewing enclosures. Grahame-White also founded the Grahame-White Aviation Company Ltd. which manufactured aircraft at Aerodrome Road. Production expanded greatly during the war and other manufacturers were attracted to the area by Government intervention. The Aircraft Manufacturing Company (Airco) had a large factory on the Kingsbury side of the Edgware Road and in 1912 Handley Page Ltd. established a factory at Cricklewood where pioneering aircraft were built and flown from the company's adjacent airfield. Hendon Aerodrome was requisitioned by the Government during the war and was in the hands of the RAF from its formation in 1918. After a bitter legal dispute the Government was forced to buy the aerodrome and factory in 1925. By then it was already used as the venue for the famous RAF pageant, and for the wider world Hendon meant the aerodrome. The last RAF pageant was held in 1937 when the airfield, enclosed by suburbia on all sides, was deemed unsuitable for intensive air activity. Fighter aircraft were briefly stationed there at the outbreak of the Second World War but by 1940 it had become a communications base and was used solely for transport and training. It finally closed to flying in 1957 and was covered by Grahame Park housing estate, which was under construction by the late 1960s. A small part did continue as the RAF Supply Control Centre until 1988 and two of the aerodrome's original hangars were used for the RAF Museum which opened in 1973.

The planned extension of the underground to Edgware resumed after the war and was completed in 1924. Four intermediate stations, Brent (later Brent Cross), Hendon Central, Colindale and Burnt Oak were opened. Once again the builders came with the track and rapid development followed – mansion houses, cottages, farms and fields were replaced by the 'little palaces' of the '20s and '30s which made Hendon part of 'semi-detached London'. These houses were immediately attractive to families moving out from the congested city and East End and notable among their owners was the number of Jewish families. The first came after the opening of the Golders Green tube, the first festivals being held in a house in West Heath Drive in 1913, but it was during the '20s that a strong community was established and the first purpose-built synagogues appeared. Numbers increased in the '30s when many fleeing the Nazis settled in the area. It was estimated in 1939 that there were over 14,000 aliens (the official term) in the Metropolitan Police 'S' division (covering

Hampstead, Golders Green, Hendon, Edgware and Mill Hill), almost a quarter of the entire alien population of Britain at the time.

Although the new housing was largely middle-class there were exceptions. The L.C.C. built its Watling estate over Goldbeaters Farm at Burnt Oak from 1926 to 1931 to house semi-skilled workers and manual labourers from inner London. Influenced by the earlier garden suburbs, it was well planned and care was taken to preserve existing trees, as well as the 45-acre open space alongside the Silk Stream. At first life on the estate was fairly bleak, but services and community life soon developed and residents from other parts of Hendon were soon visiting its shops in Watling Avenue and its market. The U.D.C. increased its house building programme and by 1932 had built over 1,000 council houses including a large estate at The Hyde, although even this did not compare in scale to Watling.

At the same time new arterial roads were driven through the area – the Hendon-Watford Way and the North Circular Road were completed in 1927 and linked by the Great North Way, completed in 1926. They helped to encourage not only the building of houses but also of factories, which were especially attracted to the North Circular.

In 1931 the parish of Edgware became part of Hendon U.D. which, with a population of 115,682, became the largest urban district in the country. This enabled Hendon to achieve borough status the following year and indulge in civic ceremonies of considerable pomp. The new borough council was soon providing new services, opening new schools and health centres and preserving open spaces for recreation. The library service was notably improved when the Central Library in The Burroughs, opened in 1929, was joined by new branches at Golders Green in 1935 and Mill Hill in 1937. The decade also saw some other significant developments. The Metropolitan Police College opened in 1935 in a building originally erected by Grahame-White as a flying club and, like the aerodrome, brought Hendon to the attention of a wider world. In 1939 Hendon Technical Institute (now part of Middlesex University) opened, but was immediately used for civil defence purposes and there were more war personnel there than students.

The council had responsibility for civil defence and, with the full support of its residents, led the local war effort, organising the A.R.P. (Air Raid Precautions), meal services and British Restaurants and doing what it could to raise morale. It also took the lead in a wide range of fund-raising campaigns, of which the most spectacular was the Four Fighter Fund which raised money to buy four Spitfires. Hendon was not, of course, the only borough to engage in such schemes, but its achievement in organising them throughout the duration of the war was outstanding. Although it did not suffer the full force of the blitz that fell on inner London and other industrialised centres, Hendon was extensively bombed. The aircraft and motor industries along the Edgware Road, the airfield, and railway lines were strategic targets, but many of the bombs fell on residential areas. The worst single incident took place at West Hendon when a V2 rocket devastated three roads, killed 80 people and left 1,500 homeless in February 1941.

The expectation of victory led to talks on post-war reconstruction both at national and local level. In Hendon such a meeting was held in March 1945 with the chief officers of the council as the main speakers, and topics such as housing and education high on the agenda. No promises were made but the speakers spoke with more optimism than certainty. The immediate post-war years were austere: food rationing continued and there were periodic shortages in basic commodities, and there were building restrictions. The latter postponed until the 1950s attempts to expand the library service, so a travelling library was introduced in 1947. The council, to its credit, did manage to build over 1,300 new homes between 1945 and 1952. These were mostly traditional house units: it was not until the late 1950s that multi-storey flats became the norm for council building, usually in redevelopments replacing properties designated as 'slum' or 'near slum'. Industrial sites in such areas were also acquired under the 1957 Housing Act and industries were relocated to land zoned for industrial purposes. In 1963 the council opened Endeavour House, a flatted factory on the North Circular designed to house various industrial concerns relocated from areas like New Brent Street and North Street in central Hendon and Granville Road in Child's Hill.

A major post-war change was the arrival of newcomers from many parts of the world, particularly the new Commonwealth, and today the area is one of the most multi-cultural in London, with a splendid range of shops and facilities which reflect this.

Radical reorganisation occurred in 1965, following the London Government Act of 1963. A more extensive Greater London area was created and placed under the G.L.C. or Greater London Council (since abolished), which replaced the old Middlesex and London County Councils. The area was also divided into 32 London Boroughs. Hendon was joined with the borough of Finchley and the urban districts of Barnet, East Barnet and Friern Barnet to form the London Borough of Barnet, which was fourth largest of the 32 in area and second in population. Hendon was the biggest of the new borough's constituent parts and had the most highly developed services, and its councillors fought a protracted, but ultimately unsuccessful, battle to give its name to the new borough. The creation of the London Borough of Barnet marks the cut-off point for this book.

The various districts which make up Hendon remain, for their residents, as distinct as they have always been, whether within the borough of Hendon or the London Borough of Barnet. It is hoped that this book will inform and entertain all who want to know more about the making of Hendon and thus increase their enjoyment of today's environment. Most of the illustrations and information come from the borough's Archives & Local Studies Centre, which is always happy to welcome all enquirers.

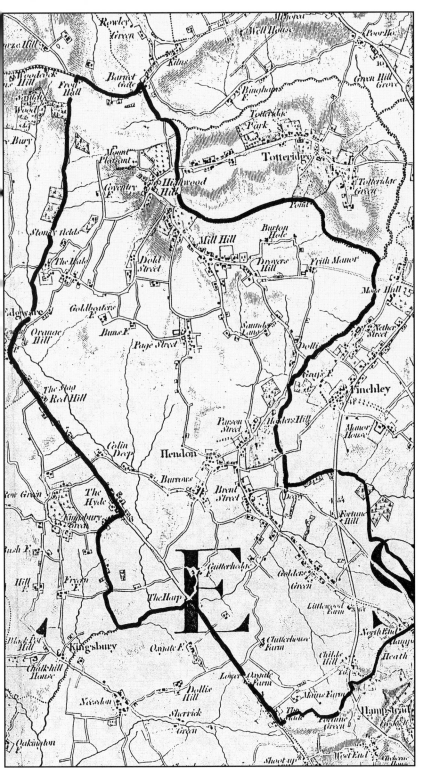

2. This is a moulded face from a Roman flagon neck, which was found at Church End in an excavation of 1973-4. Like other finds from the same dig, it belongs to the late third to early fourth centuries. There have been other Roman finds elsewhere. The Anglo-Saxon name 'Hendon' means 'at the high down' and refers to Church End's situation at the top of Greyhound Hill. This is an early placename, whose type may also indicate awareness of the pre-existing Roman settlement.

1. The area of Hendon outlined on the 1" to the mile Ordnance Survey map of 1822. (The large E and S capitals come from the word 'Middlesex'.) Despite the small scale the map gives a good idea of the street and settlement pattern at the time. There are some very good and detailed 18th-century surveys of Hendon, but they are on too large a scale for easy reproduction.

3 & 4. Beloved of print-makers and artists, St Mary's crowns the hill-top settlement. The earliest references to a church here and the earliest parts of its fabric, including the beautiful font, date to the 12th century, but there was a priest by 1086.

5. The name 'Handone' is very clear at the start of the Domesday Book entry, made in 1086. The manor belonged to the abbey of St Peter's Westminster from well before the Norman Conquest until the 16th century, when it passed into lay ownership. Hendon was a large and important manor, and from Domesday Book and a rich series of later manorial records and surveys we can discover much detail about the life of this area.

6a & b. Beating the Bounds. Perambulation of the parish boundaries to keep them in the community's memory was an important annual event. The last regular beating in Hendon took place in 1926, when the photograph was taken. The group is standing at Finchley Lane Bridge, which had been rebuilt in 1897 but was then being altered as part of the Great North Way construction.

HENDON.

The Boundaries of this Parish
WILL BE

PERAMBULATED

ON TUESDAY NEXT, AUGUST 1,
AND THURSDAY FOLLOWING, AUGUST 3, 1865.

The Procession will start from the Harp Bridge in the Edgware Road at 9 o'clock in the Morning, proceed to Woodhouse, the Hyde, Edgware Bridge, Coventry Farm, Barnet Gate, Finchley Brook, to Finchley Bridge.

On the Second Day, to start from Finchley Bridge at 10 o'clock in the Morning, proceed along Mutton Brook, Wild Lane, Weild Wood, Hampstead Heath, North End, Blacket's Well, Child's Hill, Cricklewood, along the Edgware Road to the Harp Bridge.

Persons intending to Dine at 5 o'clock at the Lower Welch Harp on the 3rd of August, are requested to signify the same previously to one of the Churchwardens, on or before Tuesday, the 1st of August.

Dated this 25th day of July, 1865.

W. F. SWEETLAND, Churchwardens.
GEORGE MORGAN,

Simpson, Printer and Bookbinder, "Chronicle" Office, Edgware.

7. The Edgware Road, or Watling Street, provides most of Hendon's western boundary. It was the Roman road from London to St Albans (Verulamium) and the north, and has been a major road ever since. Brent Bridge was also known as Harp Bridge because of the adjacent *Old* or *Lower Welsh Harp* inn, shown in this 1799 print. The inn also gave its name to the nearby reservoir, begun in the 1830s. The bridge was regularly rebuilt from at least the 18th century until it effectively vanished when the river was culverted in the 1920s.

8. The Dollis Brook forms much of Hendon's eastern boundary. The lake, seen here in about 1900, was made by a dam at Finchley Lane Bridge and stretched back to Waverley Grove. It lay within the grounds of Tenterden Hall, the former manor house, and was probably made in the second half of the 18th century. It vanished in the 1920s, when the local rivers were channelled and public riverside footpaths created.

9. Hendon Place was rebuilt *c.*1760, leaving no trace of either its Elizabethan predecessor or the medieval manor house. By the late 19th century it was known as Tenterden Hall after Charles Abbott, Lord Tenterden of Hendon, who had owned it earlier in the century. It ceased to be a residence in 1873 when it was taken over by Hendon Preparatory School. The school remained there until 1934 when the house was demolished to make way for new housing. The name lives on in the street names – Tenterden Grove, Drive and Gardens.

10. James Barber, to whom we owe many of our best pictures of Victorian Hendon, took this shot of his family in Ashley Lane *c.*1898. The lane is part of one of the many early north-south routes through Hendon, and was used by Cardinal Wolsey in 1530, riding towards York after an overnight stop at the manor house. Its deeply rural look was only slightly surprising in the 1890s, but its partial survival today is highly remarkable and due to the fields either side being developed for purposes other than housing. Hendon Park Cemetery opened on the east in 1899 and just below it in 1900 Hendon Golf Course. (Part of the latter's grounds were lost to the Great North Way in the mid-1920s, but the land west of the lane was purchased instead.)

11. Hendon House was built in the late 16th century and became home to John Norden, the Elizabethan cartographer. A succession of notable 18th-century owners followed including Sir William Rawlinson, a Commissioner of the Great Seal, and the politician, Giles Earle. This print dates to 1796, shortly before the house was rebuilt when it was owned by John Cornwall, the first Director of the Bank of England. It was demolished in 1909 and Hendon County School built on the site.

12. Copthall was built on Page Street in the early 17th century by Randall Nicoll, a member of one of Mill Hill's oldest families. They were responsible for building at least five houses of note but it is Copthall which is best remembered. This photograph from 1908 shows the courtyard and entrance. It was converted into flats in 1932, finally demolished in 1959 and replaced by a block of flats called Randall Court. The name lives on in Copthall Pool (1977) and Stadium (1964).

13. Another member of the Nicoll family, Thomas, built these almshouses facing Angel Pond in 1696, according to the stone inscription which can still be seen on their wall. Nicoll, however, did not endow them so their upkeep fell to the parish. This photograph shows them c.1893, by which time they had been improved by the addition of sculleries.

14. At the heart of Church End stands the *Greyhound Inn*, which is owned by the adjacent church and was long used for parish meetings. There has been an inn here since at least the mid-17th century, but the building was replaced soon after this picture was taken, in 1896, by the one which currently stands.

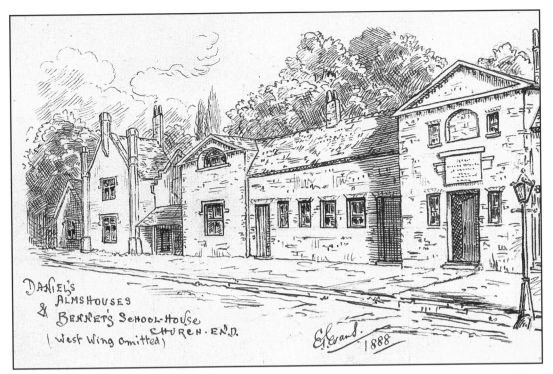

DANiEL'S
ALMSHOUSES
& BENNET'S SCHOOL-HOUSE
CHURCH-END.
(West Wing omitted)

E. Evans. 1888

15. Daniel's Almshouses and Bennet's School at Church End are shown in this ink drawing from 1888 by Edward Evans, a noted local historian. The almshouses were established in 1729 by the will of Robert Daniel, a rich city merchant, and their external appearance has changed little since they were rebuilt c.1800. The school was founded by John Bennett as a charity school in 1766. It united with the National Society in 1828 and, renamed St Mary's National School, moved to new premises at Church Walk in 1857. The old premises were then used by Hendon Baptist Church, and as a working men's club, but by 1888 were King's furniture warehouse. They were demolished in 1937.

16. Highwood House belonged to Rachel, Lady Russell after the execution of her husband, Lord William, for his alleged part in the 1683 Rye House Plot to assassinate Charles II. She is commemorated by the surviving well-head she had built over a chalybeate spring in the house's grounds. This print shows the house as it looked after rebuilding in 1817. In 1825 it was bought by Sir Stamford Raffles on his return from the East Indies. His stay, now commemorated by a blue plaque, was brief: he died in 1826, and was buried at St Mary's.

17. *The Three Crowns* on Highwood Hill was built on the Hendon Park House estate in the 17th century. Nan Clark was the licensee from *c.*1690, and her name is now given to the passage to the right of the inn, originally called Moat Mount Lane. Her ghost supposedly haunts it at midnight by full moon, though few have claimed to see her. The inn had closed before 1890, not long after this picture was taken. Thereafter the building had a period of residential use until its demolition in 1937.

18. Colindeep Lane in the early years of this century. Also known as Ancient Street, it was part of a major early route coming up via Hampstead, Golders Green Road and Brent Street which at least until the 16th century was often used by travellers in preference to the swampy southern stretch of Edgware Road. There was a ford across the Silk Stream and, by 1826, a footbridge. The southern end of the lane was incorporated into the new Watford Way in the mid-1920s, and the rest modernised when the roads on its southern side were developed in the early 1930s.

19. This was the view eastwards along Bell Lane in 1883. Decoy Farm on the right took its name from the adjacent duck decoy, which was there by the mid-18th century, and possibly long before. The old Mutton Bridge was replaced when Bell Lane was widened in 1931, and the farmhouse went in 1935. The view had already been transformed, when the North Circular was built across it in 1924.

20. Rosebank, a group of weather-boarded cottages on The Ridgeway, was used as a Quaker meeting house between 1678 and 1719 and the prominent blue plaque was erected in 1961 to commemorate this. After 1719 the building was converted into a two-storey dwelling. It was purchased by Mill Hill School as hostel accommodation in the early 1920s but soon reverted to private occupancy. After a period of serious disrepair in the 1980s it was renovated in 1990.

21. Moat Mount estate was created by the sale of all the manorial demesne lands in 1756. The sale catalogue shows as Lot 17 'The Moat Mount, an elevated piece of ground, and a proper place to build on, on account of the beautiful prospects therefrom ...'. By 1792 a large mansion had duly appeared. This postcard shows the 19th-century rebuild commissioned by Edward William Cox, whose family added considerably to the estate. In 1906 much was sold including the farms – Hiver Hill, Barnet Gate, Boys Hill, Clay and Coventry. The remainder went in 1923, part becoming Mote Mount (now Mill Hill) Golf Club, and the rest Moat Mount Countryside Park. The house was severely damaged by fire in 1934 and later reduced to the two-storey building which, as Mote Mount, still survives.

22. The Hendon Hall estate was another created by the 1756 sale. This postcard shows the hall's south front to Parson Street, which was given its Renaissance aspect in a mid-19th century alteration. It is famous for its connection with the actor-manager David Garrick, who held the lordship of Hendon manor from 1765-79. There is no evidence that he ever lived there, but the grounds did once contain many ornaments celebrating the connection, including an octagonal temple to Shakespeare. The hall became a private school in 1898 and, in 1912, enduringly, a hotel. There have been many changes and extensions since. The grounds shrank with the arrival of the Great North Way in 1926.

23. The name Golders Green is not recorded until the 17th century, but it may be related to the local 14th-century God(y)ere family, and there was certainly medieval settlement in the area. The road in this heavily idealised 1789 print is the Golders Green Road since the Finchley Road, and thus the crossroads, did not appear until the 1820s.

GOLDERS GREEN,

NEAR HENDON, MIDDLESEX,

Painted by J. Russel, R.A. & engraved by W. Birch, Enamel Painter.

Published Aug.1 1789 by W.m Birch, Hampstead Heath, & sold by T.Thornton Southampton Street, Covent Garden.

24. Woodstock House was one of a number of substantial villas built from the late 18th century on inclosures from the manorial waste land along the Golders Green Road. Originally known as Rose Cottage, it was occupied from 1816-35 by Sir Felix Booth of Booth & Co., distillers, and noted patron of an important expedition to the Arctic regions of North America. After this 1888 sale the house was sold again in 1909 to the Sisters of La Sagesse. They moved their convent school from Rock Hall, Cricklewood and over the years added various new buildings. The house is now used as the Menorah Grammar School and the other buildings by various Jewish organisations.

25. Just to the north stands *The White Swan*, originally a coaching inn first recorded in 1751. This postcard shows it before modernisation in 1913 when the present frontage was added to the original structure. The adjacent weather-boarded cottage is Grove Farm Dairy, which was demolished in 1931.

The HAPPY SHEPHERD *with a* VIEW *of* Childs Hill *Middlesex.*

London, Printed for R. Sayer & J. Bennett, Map, Chart & Printsellers, N°.53, Fleet Street, as the Act directs, October, 1st 1784.

John Peltro sculp.

26. The mountainous backdrop to this idyllic 1784 print warns us against taking it too literally. It is, however, true that Child's Hill is a substantial hill and as such was the site of an early settlement. It is probably the 10th-century *Codenhleawe* and certainly the later Cowhouse, a sub-manor sometimes disputed between the two neighbouring Westminster manors of Hendon and Hampstead. The settlement was partially destroyed, and refocused, by the building of the Finchley Road.

27. Mill Hill School was founded in 1807 as the Protestant Dissenters' Grammar School: one of several trying to meet the need for non-Anglican public schools. It opened in Ridgeway House, since demolished, and the beautiful neo-Grecian buildings shown here were built in 1825-7. There have been many later additions.

28. Among the additions was a new chapel. A very plain building was added in 1832, and replaced by the current one in 1898. The magnificent edifice shown here was apparently designed *c.*1860, but never built. The chapel also served the local community from the start until 1908, when the Congregationalists moved to former Baptist premises in Tennyson Road, and thence to Lawrence Street in 1911. Their present Union Church, though, was not built until 1936.

29. By the 1860s the school was close to collapse, but was refounded in 1869 and rapidly surged ahead under a dynamic new Head. Among the new staff was James Murray, seen here in the centre of the group. He taught here from 1870-85 while simultaneously working on his *New English Dictionary*, which became the *Oxford English Dictionary*. His house, Sunnyside, later renamed Murray House, now bears a blue plaque.

30. Hendon Poor Law Union was formed in 1835 and initially covered a huge area of eight parishes, stretching from Hendon to Pinner and Willesden. The union workhouse opened the same year in Redhill House on the Edgware Road. An adjacent infirmary opened in 1865 and the whole complex was regularly enlarged. A completely new building, Redhill Hospital, was opened in 1927, although the infirmary was still used for acute cases. When the poor law unions were abolished in 1930 Redhill passed to Middlesex County Council, which in 1938 enlarged the hospital from 200 to 700 beds and made it the most up-to-date in England. It was absorbed into the new NHS in 1948, becoming Edgware General Hospital. The old workhouse and infirmary, since 1930 the Redhill Institution, remained with the county council. The buildings were demolished in 1971 and replaced by housing for the elderly.

31. Goodyers stood on the south side of Queens Road as it turns along Brent Green, between the present Queens and Goodyer Gardens. It was already an important house with considerable lands in the Middle Ages, when it belonged to the Godere and Brent families. From 1696 until this century it belonged to the Kemps, also a major local family, who in 1774 rebuilt the house seen here. But it was often let to tenants; among them and of more than local fame was T.J. Cobden-Sanderson, the bookbinder who lived here from 1885-92. Part of Goodyers' lands, the Step Fields, were bought in 1900 to become Hendon Park. There were closer encroachments during the 1920s and the house was finally demolished in 1934.

32. Further south on the corner of Brent Street and Shirehall Lane was Albert Cottage, which seems to have been built in 1713 as an overnight house for drovers on their way to the London markets. It was purchased by the Hendon Electric Supply Co. in 1923, and their renovations revealed that it had an oak frame built from second-hand timber of considerable age, possibly from a barn or even a ship. Although the cottage's period as an overnight house was shortlived, the company renamed it 'Penfold' and commissioned the fresco of a shepherd with a lamb above the door.

RURAL SPORTS.

MONDAY, MAY 11th, 1801,

AT

THE BELL-INN, BRENT-STREET, HENDON.

To begin at 12 at Noon, precisely.

1ſt. A PIG, value 2l. 2s. to be run for, after having undergone the uſual ceremony of ſhaving and ſoaping; none but independent courſers need ſtart, as no combination will be allowed.

2d. A HOLLAND SMOCK, decorated with ribbands, value 1l. 1s. for which not leſs than four of the fair ſex are to ſtart; this diſplay of activity will gain the competitors many admirers, each *(perhaps)* a huſband, and the winner a *handſome wedding garment*; the ſecond beſt to be rewarded with a premium of five ſhillings.

3d. A SILK HANDKERCHIEF, value 8s. 6d. to be grinned for. This will afford ſuch perſons as are diſſatisfied with the cut of their faces, an opportunity of putting them into ſuch forms as they may think proper, and thoſe who pride themſelves upon expreſſive features, may turn their heads into *moving pictures*, with horſe-collars for their frames.

4th. A PAIR OF LEATHER *SMALL CLOATHS*, (vulgarly called breeches) value 1l. 11s. 6d. to be run for in Sacks; ſo that any perſon *ſure of winning* may leave his own at home, and upon quitting his ſack, march away dreſſed in the token of his victory.

5th. A jingling match for a HAT, value 10s. 6d. and a PAIR OF SHOES, value 10s. 6d. in which they that believe all that they hear, may, or may not win. Fair ſport to be adjudged by two umpires, and foul play to be puniſhed with excluſion or pitch-plaiſter.

Perſons deſirous of becoming candidates for the above prizes, are to deliver in their names, and further particulars to be known on application to ROBERT, Clerk of the Courſe,

BELL, HENDON.

STEEL, Printer, 31, Lothbury, London.

33. This bill from 1801 advertises the kind of rural sports which were popular at fairs during the late 18th and early 19th centuries. Especially notable is the first event of pig running. The pig with its tail shaved and soaped was let loose among the competitors, and the one who could seize it by the tail and throw it over his shoulders won it as a prize.

34. Mill Hill may seem to have had a disproportionate number of inns for such a small population but most of them were simply small cottages with a licence to sell ale, and often the landlords would have other occupations. *The Plough* on Holcombe Hill, shown here in the 1880s, is a typical example. It closed in 1912 and remained a private cottage until its demolition in 1931.

35. One of the small cottages adjacent to *The Plough* was home to Mrs. Cole, one-time needlewoman to Lady Raffles at Highwood House. She was 90 when this photograph was taken in 1882.

36. The tiny two-roomed Vine Cottage in Cricklewood Lane, pictured here in 1958, had been a Dame School for Child's Hill until the mid-19th century. Despite a vigorous campaign to preserve the cottage, it was demolished in 1981.

37. The Finchley Road was built as a turnpike road from 1825 to improve access to the West End. Entering Hendon at Child's Hill, it followed an entirely new route through Golders Green and Temple Fortune to Church End Finchley where it used an improved Ballards Lane to Tally Ho. There were local toll-gates at Child's Hill and Golders Green. This photograph from *c.*1906 shows the section which leads up the hill to Temple Fortune. This replaced Ducksetters Lane, the old route to Church End Finchley, which had vanished from the maps by the 1860s.

38. The arrival of the new road brought some growth to Temple Fortune: the *Royal Oak*, shown here in this early 20th-century postcard, was established to serve the coaching traffic, and some terraces of cottages appeared by the mid-19th century. However, the area remained rural until the early 1900s when development followed improved transport links, and the neighbouring Hampstead Garden Suburb, built east of Temple Fortune, was under construction.

9a & b. Theodore Williams (right) was Hendon's vicar from 1812-75. Famously combatant, he nevertheless failed to prevent the anti-slavery campaigner William Wilberforce, then resident at Hendon Park, from building the first new Anglican chapel within Hendon. The Bishop of London and the Ecclesiastical Commissioners supported Wilberforce, but the opening of St Paul's in 1833 occurred after his death. The postcard of the church (below) was sent in 1904.

40. Theodore Williams created a garden at the Vicarage much cited throughout the 1830s as a model of what could be achieved (with several gardeners) on a small (1½-acre) scale. It was still magnificent in 1904 when this picture was taken. Today the attractive early 19th-century house on Parson Street remains, but shorn of almost all its grounds.

41. Until 1866, when the West Middlesex Waterworks Co. was empowered to provide piped water, the southern part of Hendon was supplied from this parish pump, which stood at the junction of Brent Street and Bell Lane. The print dates from 1828.

42. Agnes Beattie Holgate, who painted many fine watercolours of a now-vanished Hendon, painted this one c.1850. It shows Samuel Ware of Hendon Hall riding north from Brent Bridge past Brent Green. The green, the last piece of manorial waste in southern Hendon, was saved from development in 1878 and is still preserved as a small open space.

43. Farmer Nathan Bell and his family at Belmont Farm on The Ridgeway during the 1880s. The farm, like most in the district, was given over to the production of hay, which was needed to feed London's huge horse population. Mill Hill in particular was noted for its good quality hay and these haystacks display the fine thatching typical of Middlesex farms.

44. The hay-harvest brought large numbers of itinerant labourers into the parish, especially from Ireland. Their presence, in addition to that of resident Catholics, attracted a mission from the Passionist Fathers, who were active in the area from the 1840s, and based at Woodfield House, shown here before its demolition in 1940, from 1852-8. Their plans to build an elaborate monastery on the site proved abortive, so they moved to Highgate Hill and the house passed into private ownership. The site is now occupied by Woodfield Nurseries.

45. The Catholic chapel of Our Lady of Dolours, standing in splendid isolation. It was built in 1863, replacing an 1850 hut, and remodelled in 1927. The turret has now gone and Egerton Gardens, built c.1910, passes to the left. Access was from Chapel Walk, on the right, whose name probably comes from an even earlier (1827) Methodist chapel.

46. The impossibility of St Mary's church continuing to cover so huge a parish became increasingly obvious during the 19th century. Nevertheless it was not until 1856 that All Saints Child's Hill was consecrated, replacing the laundry which had previously been used. The church is seen here in the early 20th century, after aisles and transepts were added in 1878-84, but before the severe fire damage of 1940 and restoration of 1952.

47. The Midland Line from London to Bedford opened for goods in 1867 and for passengers in 1868, when stations opened at Hendon, Mill Hill and Cricklewood. There was also a Welsh Harp station from 1870-1903. Commuter services were few, and the line did little to hasten suburban development.

48. Similarly the G.N.R.'s branch line from Finsbury Park to Edgware, which opened in 1867, did little to stimulate growth. There were local stations at Mill Hill (later Mill Hill East), and from 1906 at The Hale, shown here in its first year. The new halt proved unpopular even after suburbanisation in the 1920s, and was closed in 1939. The line was electrified in 1941, but only as far as Mill Hill East. The continuation to Edgware was opened only to freight after 1939 and finally abandoned in 1964.

OSEPHS COLLEGE
ILL HILL.

49. In 1866 Cardinal Vaughan founded the Society of Foreign Missioners and bought Holcombe House to house himself and the first students until St Joseph's could be built. This took from 1869-73 and the imposing tower topped by a statue of St Joseph, one of the landmarks of Mill Hill, also marked the college's completion. Holcombe House, at Cardinal Vaughan's instigation, passed to a congregation of Franciscan nuns of the Regular Third Order in 1881, and was renamed St Mary's Abbey.

50. St Vincent's was the last of the trinity of Catholic institutions which came to Mill Hill from 1866 onwards. The British Province of the Sisters of Charity of St Vincent de Paul bought 17th-century Littleberries in 1885 and additions began almost immediately. Among their other activities, the sisters ran a boy's orphanage from 1887-1971, in which this picture was taken *c*.1932. The ownership by these institutions and Mill Hill School of large tracts of land has enabled the village to escape speculative developers, and even today it retains a rural gentrified air.

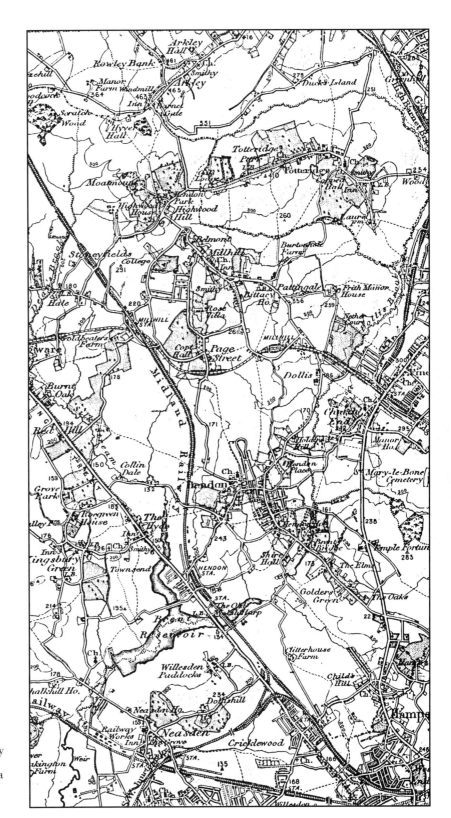

51. The Hendon section of the Ordnance Survey 1" map of North London, 1896. By this date some of the early settlements are beginning to join together and suburban growth at Cricklewood, Child's Hill, West Hendon and Brent Street is particularly evident (compare with plate 1). However, much of the area remains rural.

52. Brent Street's population expanded rapidly from the 1870s as working-class terraces developed both east and west of the road. *The Rose and Crown*, shown here *c.*1872, was opened to serve them. This stood opposite Brent Street's junction with New Brent Street until it was destroyed to make way for the Sentinel Square shopping and office complex in 1970.

53. The population growth also brought The Institution (the church-like building in the centre of the picture), which opened in 1875, just north of Brent Street's junction with Brampton Grove. It provided accommodation for concerts, bazaars and public meetings until 1906, when it became a G.P.O. sorting office. The three-storey building seen beyond is Hendon Police Station, which opened in 1884 replacing an earlier one established in a cottage in New Brent Street. The station is still in use, although the upper floors are no longer used as married quarters.

54. This early 19th-century print shows Gothic Cottage at Holders Hill. It was demolished and replaced by Holders Hill House, one of several villas built by C. F. Hancock in the Parson Street area in the 1870s. The villa survived the inter-war suburbanisation by becoming home to Ravensfield College in 1931 and since 1947 it has formed the central part of the Hasmonean Boys School.

55. Colonel Bacon and family in the grounds of Tudor House in 1902. The house, one of Hancock's villas, still stands at the junction of Parson Street and Tenterden Grove, but the grounds have gone.

The Tower, St. Swithin's, Hendon, GEORGE HORNBLOWER, Architect.

56. Another of the surviving Parson Street villas is St Swithin's and this illustration from the *Building News* records the extensions of *c*.1900. The house was bought by the Poor Sisters of Nazareth in 1932 and renamed Nazareth House. It now a base for the Montford Missionaries.

57. Sunningfields Crescent, shown here in 1901, was one of central Hendon's fairly upmarket Victorian developments. The road layout was completed in 1871 and the sites of these houses auctioned in 1879 for the building of 'superior detached or semi-detached villa residences'. The estate was built on part of the Sunny Fields, from which it took its street names.

58. The Dowding family of Brook Lodge in the 1890s. The building, originally an 18th-century farmhouse, was converted to this gentleman's residence shortly before 1828. It stood just south of Brent Bridge and was used from the 1920s as an annexe to the neighbouring *Brent Bridge Hotel*. The house was demolished in 1935, bequeathing its name to the large block of flats which replaced it.

59a & b. Sports and other recreational clubs flourished among the more prosperous residents of late Victorian Hendon. The above photo shows members of the Sunningfields Lawn Tennis Club, and the one below shows the Hendon Athletic Sports Club, which was initially run by the Hendon Cricket and Football Clubs. Both pictures were taken around the 1890s.

60. Shooting was also popular and there were rifle ranges at the Welsh Harp and at Child's Hill. This postcard records the inauguration of Hendon and Cricklewood Rifle Club by Field-Marshal Earl Roberts, V.C. in 1906.

61a & b. Miss Goode enjoying the gardens of Burroughs Lodge in 1901 when it was owned by J. Crawford Bromehead, a magistrate and churchwarden of St Mary's. Among the delights of its extensive ornamental grounds was the swan lake seen in the bottom picture. The site is now occupied by Richmond Gardens.

62. The Burroughs Pond may not have been as grand as the Burroughs Lodge lake, but its scenic qualities were appreciated by artists and commercial photographers alike. It was effectively destroyed by the coming of the Watford Way in the 1920s. The low white buildings on the right had been the parish cottages annexed to the old parish workhouse, which stood behind them. All were demolished in 1934 and replaced by Quadrant Close.

63. This photograph, taken in the 1890s, shows the opposite side of The Burroughs. The small shop in the centre was then run by Thomas Hudson, a plumber, and ballcocks, basins, pipes and other equipment essential to his trade can be seen in the shop window. The building survives, as does the attractive group of 18th-century houses to the left. Grove Terrace, to the right, was demolished in the mid-1960s and replaced by a car park.

WELSH HARP FISHERY.

THE ABOVE FISHERY IS FORMED BY THE KINGSBURY RESERVOIR, AND IS PLEASANTLY SITUATED, ON THE EDGWARE ROAD FIVE MILES FROM THE MARBLE ARCH, AND TWO FROM KILBURN STATION OF THE HAMPSTEAD JUNCTION, FORMING A MOST BEAUTIFUL LAKE OF 350 ACRES OF WATER BESIDES TRIBUTARY STREAMS UPWARDS OF 8 MILES ROUND. IT IS WELL STOCKED AND PRESERVED AND ABOUNDS WITH LARGE

PIKE, PERCH, CARP, TENCH, ROACH, CHUB, BREAM, EELS, &c. &c.

LIVE BAITS AND FISHING PUNTS MAY BE OBTAINED.

BREAKFASTS FROM SIX IN THE MORNING.

AN ORDINARY ON SUNDAYS AT ½ PAST ONE O'CLOCK
AT 1S PER HEAD

A SPLENDID PAVILION CAPABLE OF DINING 250 PERSONS.

OFFERING EVERY ACCOMMODATION, FOR SOCIETIES DINNERS, BEAN FEASTS, SCHOOLS, &c

WINES SPIRITS AND MALT LIQUORS OF THE VERY FINEST QUALITY

TICKETS TO BE OBTAINED, AT THE LOWER WELSH HARP ADJOINING THE FISHERY, WHERE ANGLERS WILL FIND EVERY ACCOMMODATION

Subscription To The Fishery

ANNUALLY _____ £1 1 0
DAY TICKET FOR JACK OR PERCH _____ 2 6
DITTO BOTTOM FISHING _____ 1 0

ROWING BOATS, SAILING BOATS, BOWLING GREEN, QUOITS, SKITTLES, CRICKET, SHOOTING, BILLIARDS, & BAGATELLE.

OMNIBUSES AT SHORT INTERVALS DAILY, AND EVERY ½ HOUR ON SUNDAYS.

Good Stabling Loose Boxes, Stalls, Coach Houses and every accommodation for Horses.

W P. WARNER PROPRIETOR.

64. The Brent (or Kingsbury) Reservoir was built in the 1830s to supply water to the canal system, was extended in the 1850s, and has shrunk since. Its main fame has been as a Victorian pleasure resort, under Jack Warner the proprietor of the *Old* (or *Lower*) *Welsh Harp*, who developed a huge range of activities. The resort declined in the 1890s when the area ceased to be attractively rural. The inn was rebuilt in 1938 and survived until 1971 when it was demolished for Staples Corner flyover.

65a & b. The many sporting activities at the reservoir often reached the pages of journals like the *Illustrated Sporting and Dramatic News*, and drawings like these were often featured in the reports. The first shows the London Swimming Club's Aquatic Festival in 1870, while the second shows wrestling on Good Friday, probably from around the same time.

J. SCHWEPPE & CO LTD
NEW WORKS at HENDON opened 1896

Schweppe's
SODA WATER,
LEMONADE,
SELTZER, POTASS,
TONIC GINGER ALE,

Have always had the Patronage of Royalty,
and continue to be supplied to

Her Majesty the Queen.

ALWAYS ORDER
Whisky & Schweppe,
OR
Brandy & Schweppe.

SCHWEPPE'S Limited,
Head Office: 51, Berners Street, **LONDON**.

66. Schweppes began production at its Hendon factory in 1895, the site being chosen for proximity to the Edgware Road and Midland Railway station. Its establishment boosted development at West Hendon: the company itself providing Deerfield Cottages to house the families of 50 of its employees. In 1970 it was said to be one of the largest factories of its kind, but changing production and distribution patterns, and demands, eventually brought the factory to the end of its useful life in 1980.

67. This picture of the late Victorian *Cricklewood Tavern* in Cricklewood Lane, taken *c.*1915, is still very recognisable. Unlike many of the area's other pubs it did not undergo extensive rebuilding in the '20s or '30s. However, sadly, it has lost its splendid lamps. Cricklewood Terrace, seen beyond the inn, is also still standing.

68. St Peter's Cricklewood was dedicated in 1891, replacing an earlier mission church. This charming photograph was taken *c.*1905. The church was demolished and rebuilt in the 1970s, but closed in 1983 due to falling attendances.

St Saviour's Homes,
Hendon.

69. St Saviour's Homes, Brent Street, was opened as a home for 'feeble minded' women by the Church Army in 1897. In 1926 it was purchased by the Pillar of Fire Society, which established a bible college, school and chapel there, renaming the buildings after their American founder, Alma White.

70. Brampton Grove was put through c.1890 and a few substantial houses began to be built along it, but the process was not completed until the 1920s.

71. This peaceful view shows the now-vanished Butchers Lane in 1895. Indeed the name had already officially gone, altered to Queens Road for Victoria's jubilee in 1887. In fact it took longer to die, and is still used on the O.S. map of 1896. This stretch, though, is not today's Queens Road but the northern part which in the 1920s was incorporated into the new Watford Way. At the same time the bend shown here became Hendon Central Circus.

72. Even the main roads were often unmetalled until this century. This picture of Edgware Road being surfaced north of the Silk Bridge was taken in 1903.

73a & b. The upper picture shows Goldbeaters Farm in 1887, and the lower one of the dining room, though taken in 1927 shortly before demolition, records a perfect Victorian interior. The farm had a long and interesting history: it is probably the land in Hendon held by John the Goldbeater in 1321 and in 1859 it was bought by James Marshall, co-founder of Marshall and Snellgrove. In 1924 it was sold to the L.C.C. as part of the site for the Watling estate.

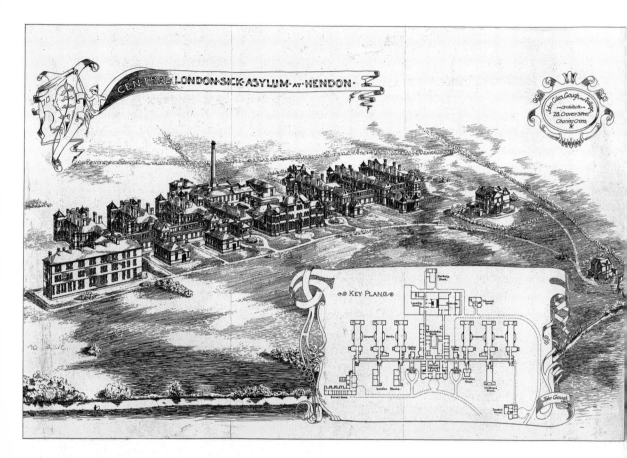

74. The tranquil rural aspect of Colindale at the turn of the century encouraged the foundation of Colindale Hospital in 1898. This was established to provide medical attention to the sick poor of the Central London Sick Asylum District, hence its original name.

75. Mill Hill village clustered at the junction of Milespit Hill and The Ridgeway. At the time of this postcard, in the early years of this century, it boasted a fair range of shops including the crenellated bakery. This and the adjacent cottages behind the trees were demolished by Mill Hill School in the 1960s. Early 18th-century Blenheim Steps, the imposing building beyond, survived as the school's shop until becoming a private house in 1978.

76. There were various other small settlements along The Ridgeway, and facilities such as pubs and shops were therefore also spread. This early 20th-century view along the 'High Street' shows Boltons Stores, which was also the village post office. It is still a shop, but not a village store. Also called the Mill House, the 18th-century building may be on the site of the mill complex.

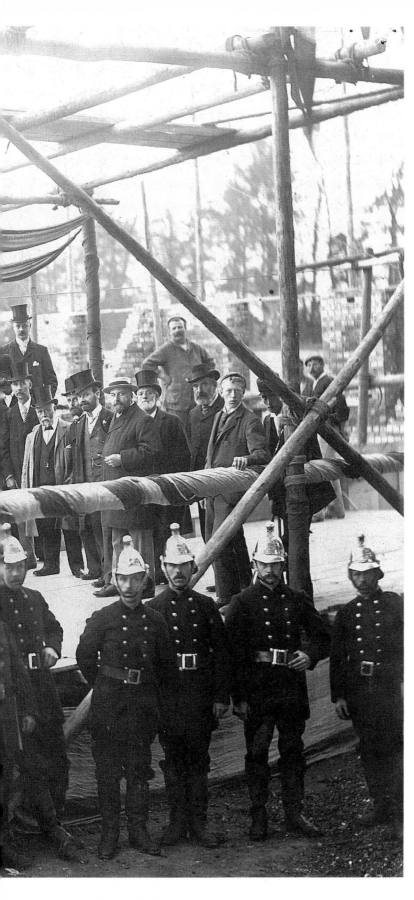

77. This photograph records the laying of the foundation stone for the new offices of the Hendon U.D.C. (Urban District Council) in 1900. It had previously met at the old parish workhouse building, where the conditions had been cramped and somewhat lacking in civic dignity. The new building was designed to reflect the U.D.C.'s growing importance to the community. It now forms the central portion of the Town Hall for the London Borough of Barnet.

78. Hendon's first fire brigade was formed in 1855 and was refounded as Hendon Volunteer Fire Brigade in 1866. This photograph dates to c.1880 when the horse-drawn engine was kept in a purpose-built garage at Church End. There were also subsidiary fire stations at Mill Hill and Child's Hill. The U.D.C. took over the responsibility for the fire service in 1899 and immediately expanded it, opening additional sub-stations at Burnt Oak, West Hendon and Golders Green in 1900. The latter two were closed in 1922 and 1927 respectively, after the large Central Fire Station at The Burroughs was opened in 1914, which also superseded the engine-house at Church End.

79. An electric lighting order for Hendon was granted to a private company in 1899, but the powers were transferred to the U.D.C. in the same year. The scheme encountered strong local opposition, evident in this election campaign handbill from 1902. Messrs. Hearn and Townsend, supported by the Hendon Ratepayers Protection Committee, were duly elected, but the progressives on the council prevailed.

MAY 4 1904

80. The houses of Golders Hill Terrace were built *c.*1890 as a curiously isolated and urban row half way along the otherwise undeveloped North End Road. The houses which followed the coming of the railway in 1907 (three years after this photo) were in a very different style.

81. The 18th-century mansion, Golders Hill House, and its beautifully landscaped grounds were bought by the L.C.C. in 1898 to create Hendon's first public park. This postcard from 1915 shows the popular tea terrace there. The house was bomb damaged in 1940 and had to be demolished, but tea is still enjoyed, particularly on Sunday afternoons, at the more modest café which replaced it.

82. Celebrations for Edward VII's coronation taking place in June 1902 at Sunny Hill Fields. Some of the fields, which belonged to Church End Farm, were built on both earlier and later, but 16 acres were sold to the council in 1921 to become Sunny Hill Park, with enlargement up to 50 acres during the following decade.

83. Hoop Lane, *c.*1915. On the right is Golders Green Crematorium, the first in London, opened in 1902 by the London Cremation Society. By the 1930s over a quarter of all cremations in Britain were being performed there. Among the many celebrities have been such diverse talents as Neville Chamberlain, Sigmund Freud, Bram Stoker, Marie Stopes and local resident Anna Pavlova. The fence opposite encloses the Jewish Cemetery founded by Sephardi Jews and the West London Reform Synagogue in 1895. The fact that the area later became popular with Jewish families was purely coincidental.

84. Dollis Farm on Holders Hill Road was at the southern edge of an early settlement, Dollis, which lay at the junction of Dollis Road and Bittacy Hill – later known as Kelly's Corner. Jeremy Bentham found the farm an ideally secluded retreat and lived and wrote in a rented room there for long periods from 1788. Some of its fields became the Hendon Park Cemetery, which opened in 1899, but the farmhouse survived until shortly after the death in 1930 of its last tenant, Thomas Whiting, who is seen in this photo.

85. This was Bittacy Farm, on Bittacy Hill opposite Sanders Lane. The postcard comes from much the same time, 1902, that the farm and its lands were sold to the War Office for the erection of barracks for the Middlesex Regiment. Some of the farm buildings nevertheless remained – indeed the final walls were not cleared until 1965.

86. Further up the hill a military funeral procession winds its way past the courtyard of Mill Hill East station (on the left). The Inglis Barracks are just visible at the top of the hill. Opened from 1905, their name came from Colonel Inglis who, while dying from his wounds at the Battle of Albuhera in the Peninsula War, rallied his men with the call 'Die hard, my men', thus giving the name 'Diehards' to the regiment.

87. This photograph from c.1905 shows the Avenue, the thoroughfare which led from Cricklewood Lane to the farm variously known as Cowhouse, Avenue or Dickers. The farm was originally 120 acres in extent but was encroached upon from all sides until the farmhouse stood alone by the time of its demolition in December 1931. The lane was suburbanised and renamed Farm Avenue.

88. An early 20th-century postcard showing Cook's Corner at the junction of Church Road and Parson Street. The corner took its name from Cook's Builders & Decorators whose premises are seen here. The junction was renamed The Quadrant in the 1920s. (Compare with plate 148.)

CHURCH ROAD HENDON

89. 1-3 Vine Cottages, seen here in 1912, stood at the top of Greyhound Hill until they were demolished in 1935. As the local paper of the time noted: 'Church End, almost the last of Hendon to change, has changed at last. Frailty added its argument to incompatibility and the death warrant of Vine Cottages was signed ...'.

90. This was Salisbury Plain or Place – an inn and row of cottages behind the corner of Brent Street and Shirehall Lane – in 1912. The inn, the *Load of Hay*, was rebuilt in grander style in 1923, but the cottages survived until the late 1940s.

91. *The Green Man* at The Hale, seen here in *c.*1908 when it was still a well known venue for sportsmen – especially greyhound racers – and picnickers. In existence since at least the 18th century, it was rebuilt in the 1930s and renamed Everglades in 1983.

92. Cricklewood Broadway, *c.1912*. *The Crown* inn was rebuilt *c.1898* on the site of an earlier Crown, which had existed since at least the mid-18th century and was famous for its pleasure grounds. The parade of shops beyond the inn was built *c.1905* on the site of one of Cricklewood's few mansions, Cricklewood House. Its last residents had been the Ropers, owners of the Kilburn Bon Marché.

93. The original *Castle* inn, there by the mid-18th century, was built on Hermitage Lane, but found itself by the junction with Finchley Road when this was driven through Child's Hill in the 1820s. The current inn was built in the 1890s. The picture may have been taken in 1906 when the numbered bus service began; trams – and therefore overhead wires – ran from 1909.

94. A postcard sent in 1909 showing Wyldes Farm, which lies just on the Hendon side of the border at Hampstead's North End. The farm has hosted many famous residents, including Dickens, and their friends. To prevent a proposed station there, some of its lands were bought in 1905 to become the Heath Extension. Soon after the rest became the site of Hampstead Garden Suburb whose architect, Raymond Unwin, moved into the farm. Amazingly the buildings, the track, and the sense of isolation, survive today.

95. The view across Golders Green crossroads towards Temple Fortune in 1906. Ernest Owers, whose temporary offices dominate the scene, was already actively developing the area in anticipation of the new railway line, which opened as far as Golders Green in 1907 and, until the 1920s, terminated there.

96. This photograph shows The Promenade, the first of several smart shopping parades and flats which sprang up at the centre of Golders Green soon after the opening of the station. They were immediately successful, not least because of the absence of all commercial facilities in the adjacent Hampstead Garden Suburb.

97. Golders Green Hippodrome opened on Boxing Day 1913. It had one of the largest proscenium arches in London and seating for 3,500. From 1913-22 it was run largely as a music hall but with some films, and thereafter until closure in 1968 it was used for touring theatre productions and occasionally ballet and opera. Since then it has been used as a BBC recording studio. The forecourt of the adjacent Golders Green station can be seen beyond the theatre in this postcard, which dates to December 1932, when *Musical Chairs* with John Gielgud had arrived direct from the Criterion.

98. This was the view along Willifield Way from Asmuns Hill, probably in 1915. Even here, in one of Hampstead Garden Suburb's more modest streets, variety is provided not just by the prospect of Central Square but also by different house styles and staggered building lines and road junctions.

99. The club house on Willifield Green opened in 1910 and provided a hall and rooms which were the focus of community life. When this photo was taken, in February 1916, it was being used as a military hospital. It was demolished by bombing in 1940.

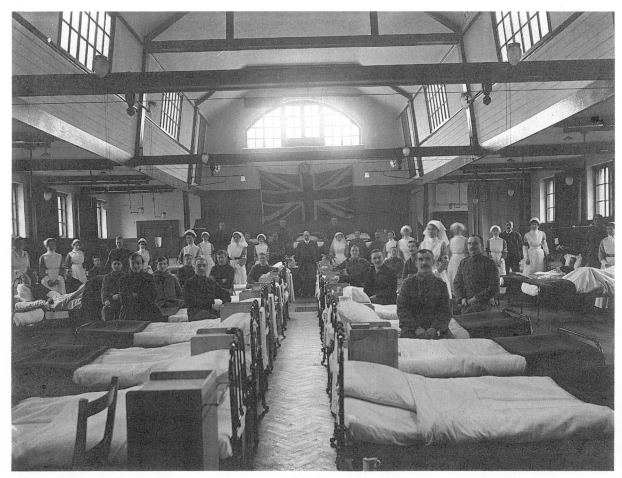

100. Another building used as a temporary military hospital was Spalding Hall in Victoria Road. It was built by the Hendon Congregationalists in 1901 and named after Thomas Spalding, one of their founder members. Their church, nearby in Brent Street, was demolished in 1980, but the hall survives and is used as offices for several commercial concerns.

101. Thomas Spalding also built Highfield, just north of the *White Swan*, in 1862. It later became a school for young ladies run by the Misses Metcalfe. The grounds were extensive and included pleasure gardens, a chapel and several outbuildings. In 1914 the house became the offices of the Workers' Union (later the T.G.W.U.) until it was demolished in 1931 for Highfield Gardens.

102. Almost opposite stood Melvin Hall which, originally called 'Little Highfield', had served as an annexe for the school. In 1912 it was sold to the Melvin Hall Cooperative Housekeeping and Service Society and named after its secretary, Alice Melvin. She had initiated the first such cooperative living experiment in London at Brent Garden Village, Finchley in 1910. The experiment here consisted of 30 serviced flats with communal kitchen and dining room, and it proved successful – communal meals were served until the society was dissolved in 1964 and the building demolished. It was replaced by a block of flats which retain the old name.

103. Intended as a memorial to Edward VII, Hendon Cottage Hospital was opened in 1913 on a greenfield site adjacent to Park Road. However, as this photograph from *c.*1927 shows, its tranquility was soon shattered by the arrival of the Hendon Way, and the large-scale residential development which followed the opening of the nearby Hendon underground station in 1923. The hospital was extended in 1925 and 1933, and with the advent of the N.H.S. in 1948 was renamed Hendon District Hospital. It closed in 1987 and demolition began in 1992. Special needs housing is planned for its site.

104. Famous for its pioneering treatment of industrial injuries, the Manor House Hospital at Golders Hill was first opened by the Allied Hospital Benevolent Society in 1917 to treat First World War victims. It was then transferred to the Industrial Orthopedic Society in 1919. This photograph records the visit of a group from the Society's Midlands area sometime in the 1920s. The old building, shown here, was originally an 18th-century mansion. It was demolished in 1962 to make way for a new four-storey wing, which opened in 1969.

105. Almost opposite stands Ivy House, which was built in the late 18th century but considerably enlarged and altered in the nineteenth. C. R. Cockerell, who lived there from 1840-51, added the frieze seen here, a cast of the Greek original he had discovered at Bassae which went to the British Museum. The most famous resident was Anna Pavlova, from 1910 until her death in 1931. She converted the library with its frieze into her dining room, which is pictured here. On her death the house was sold to Manor House Hospital, which sold it in 1962 to the New College of Speech and Drama, later part of Middlesex Polytechnic (now Middlesex University).

106. The view along the fully developed West Hendon Broadway, c.1914. The bus on the right is on Route 58 – Hendon Upper Welsh Harp to Shoreditch. This route was shortlived – introduced in 1913, it was withdrawn as a result of cuts made during the First World War and its last day of operation was 30 January 1915.

107. Claude Grahame-White, the pioneer aviator, was already one of the fashionable idols of the day, as this autographed postcard suggests, before he founded his London (or Hendon) Aerodrome at Colindale in 1910. A skilled entrepreneur, he soon turned Hendon into one of the country's leading airfields, and a major centre for the training of pilots.

108. Visitors were attracted to the aerodrome in their thousands to see events such as air races and exhibition flying. There were spectacular stunts including, as this programme from 1912 shows, illuminated night flying. Excellent facilities for the visitors were soon developed and the aerodrome became established on the social circuit, a rival to Ascot and Epsom.

GRAND ILLUMINATED
NIGHT FLYING
AND FIREWORK DISPLAY

HENDON

Thursday Evening, Sept. 26th, at 8 p.m.

Illuminated Aeroplanes piloted by well-known Aviators.

16

NEXT WEEK.

Reprinted.

NIGHT FLYING AT HENDON.

ILLUMINATED NIGHT FLIGHTS.

"WAR IN THE AIR."

On Thursday evening, September 26th, there will take place at the London Aerodrome, Hendon, what may perhaps be termed the most remarkable aerial demonstration of the year.

The usual Thursday exhibition flights will be given from 3 o'clock in the afternoon, and 8 p.m. (weather permitting), will see the commencement of the First Illuminated Flying Fete

The lighting effects will be carried out on a most extensive and hitherto unsurpassed scale, and the Aerodrome will present a perfect blaze of light. Each of the aeroplanes, which will be piloted by well-known Aviators, will carry a powerful searchlight, in addition to side and rear lights and they will also be outlined with hundreds of C.A.V. electric lights supplied from portable accumulators carried in the body of the machine. On the roofs of the hangars there will be powerful naval searchlights to guide the Airmen flying in the darkness above and the pylons which mark out the 1½ miles speed course will also be brilliantly illuminated. The various enclosures and the bandstand will also be fitted with many hundreds of coloured lanterns and the Aerodrome will present a remarkably novel and beautiful scene.

During the evening there will be a display of fire balloons and fireworks, illustrating "War in the Air," and the effect produced cannot fail to prove extremely interesting and impressive.

Amongst the Aviators who will pilot the illuminated machines are Messrs. R. T. Gates, Marcel Desoutter, Lewis Turner, Jules Nardini, Louis Noel, and J. L. Travers.

On the Saturday following (September 28th), the Naval and Military Meeting will be held.

17

109. The fields at the top of Greyhound Hill provided a popular cheap view of the aerodrome's spectaculars. Until the building of the Watford Way, Greyhound Hill was part of Hall Lane, which turned to continue north up to Page Street. This photograph was taken *c.*1912.

110. Grahame-White also founded the Grahame-White Aviation Co. which manufactured aircraft at Aerodrome Road, and expanded rapidly in response to wartime demand. Other manufacturers were also attracted to the area by Government wartime intervention and this led to the immediate transformation of rural Colindale. The photograph shows employees leaving the factory of the Aircraft Manufacturing Co. (Airco) in the Edgware Road c.1917. The fast increase in the number of aircraft workers caused the transport problems seen here: workers are crowded onto the back of a steam lorry and trailer alongside equally crowded trams.

111. After the war the Grahame-White factory's order book dropped disastrously and the company quickly diversified into building motor car bodies, as seen here, and also furniture-making. This period of activity was shortlived as a protracted dispute between Grahame-White and the Government ended with the latter buying the factory complex in 1925. The aerodrome itself had been in the hands of the RAF since its formation in 1918 and was never derequistioned.

112. Grahame-White's factory can be seen beyond the airfield in this photograph taken at the Victory Aerial Derby in 1919. From 1920-37 the aerodrome was the venue for the famous annual RAF pageant. But the site was increasingly constricting; fighter aircraft were stationed there from the outbreak of the Second World War only until 1940, when it became a communications base, and it was finally closed to flying in 1957. The RAF Supply Control Centre remained there until 1988, but the airfield was covered by the Grahame Park housing estate, completed by the early 1970s. However, the RAF Museum, which cleverly utilised two of the Grahame-White hangars, has provided a spectacular reminder of Hendon's aviation history since it opened in 1973.

The Hyde, N. W.

113. Encouraged by the combination of the Edgware Road and the aerodrome, The Hyde also expanded as an industrial centre during the 1914-18 war. There had already been some 19th-century development, notably the Hendon Brewery whose chimney dominates this pre-1910 postcard. The brewery is first recorded in 1862 under Arthur Crooke, who after major fires in 1878 and 1897 sold it to Michell & Aldous. They sold it to Trumans in 1920, who ceased to brew there in the 1950s. The site was redeveloped as Hyde House in the mid-1960s.

114. The moment of the unveiling of the Hendon War Memorial at the junction of Watford Way, The Burroughs and Station Road on St George's Day 1922. The Memorial was resited just south of the junction in 1962 as part of a Watford Way improvement scheme.

HENDON. WAR. MEMORIAL. 1

115. Hendon's pioneering aerodrome meant that many early aerial photographs were taken of the surrounding area. This dramatic early view shows the Silk Stream widening into the Welsh Harp in 1922. Most of the fields vanished in the 1920s, while the late Victorian streets of West Hendon showing here were largely demolished during and after the Second World War.

116. Despite new railway lines in the 1860s, suburban development at Mill Hill held fire until the turn of the century. Shops were built from 1910 at the lower end of Lawrence Street, and these soon became known as The Broadway. The road name changed officially in the 1920s, when the Watford Way severed this stretch from the rest of Lawrence Street. The imposing Roman Catholic church was built in 1923.

GOODWYN AVENUE,

MILL HILL GARDEN ESTATE,
LONDON, N.W.

SPECIAL MODERN CONVENIENCES.
ELECTRIC LIGHT AND BELLS.
GAS LAID ON.
PERFECT SANITATION.

Prices from
£440
Leasehold.

THESE attractive detached and semi-detached Residences — surrounded by country which is famed for its luxuriantly wooded and picturesque scenery — are built by Contract and fitted with every convenience.

They may be purchased Freehold or Leasehold, for Cash or Deposit, with balance spread over a term of years with repayments about equal to their Rental Value.

The Houses contain 2 Reception Rooms, 3 or 4 Bedrooms, Bathroom, Kitchen and usual offices.

Large Gardens, 100 feet long, properly laid out and turfed back and front.

Modern Decorations to suit purchasers' individual tastes.

The Avenue is laid out ornamentally with grass margins, planted with various kinds of Trees, alongside the footpath.

HOUSES CAN BE DESIGNED AND BUILT TO ORDER. (NO EXTRA CHARGE.)
ASK YOUR SURVEYOR TO INSPECT.

Apply: GEO. JACKSON,
Contractor,
Goodwyn Avenue,
on the Estate ;
or, 4 Wilmington Avenue, Chiswick. W.
'Phone: Chiswick 710.

117. The Mill Hill Garden Estate was one of several which, during the 1920s, covered the fields and shifted the heart of Mill Hill from The Ridgeway down to The Broadway. The houses' attractions are clearly described.

118. Mill Hill was traversed by a surprising number of lanes. Most survive, though often much altered, but the lower section of Lilley Lane, seen here probably in the early 1920s, is now only a short-distance footpath. There is another survival just left of the picture: Maxwelton, a house which since 1927 has been part of a school (first Catholic, now Jewish). A survey in 1988 revealed it contains the 17th-century timber frame and 18th-century wing of Shakerham Farm, previously assumed to have been demolished.

119. The initial stage of Elliot Road, part of the Neeld estate near Hendon Central developed in the early 1920s. Like many of the other street names on the estate, 'Elliot' commemorates a member of the Neeld family.

120. The extension of the railway beyond Golders Green to Edgware and the associated developments attracted a lot of interest and therefore a lot of dated photographs. This shot of Hendon Central was taken on 10 November 1923, nine days before the station opened.

121. The stretch of Watford Way beyond Hendon Central Circus had recently been built along Butchers Lane when this photo was taken in 1928, and shops were rapidly lining its sides. The island site with the pond and war memorial has been refashioned several times; the houses at its southern tip were demolished in the 1940s.

122. While local farms remained they benefited from the expanding demand for milk. The photo shows a Burroughs Farm delivery cart before 1920. The milkman, Thomas Kitson, not untypically transferred to working on the buses in the 1920s.

123a & b. These two cards, sent in 1920 and 1925 respectively, supply a detailed panorama of the junction of Brent Street and Bell Lane. This was an important bus terminus and, particularly before the development of Hendon Central, very much the district's focal point. The *Bell* inn at the top of Bell Lane existed by the 1750s and was remodelled after a fire in the 1960s. Most of the view on both sides of the *Bell* was removed *c.*1970 for the Sentinel Square redevelopment.

124. Cricklewood Broadway developed as a shopping area around 1900 but the magnificent Queens Hall cinema, which opened in 1920, was still quite new when this view up Cricklewood Lane was taken. Built on the site of Rock Hall, it became a Gaumont in the 1930s and was demolished in 1960. Among the many signs on Wheatlands is one to the Home of Rest for Horses, housed beyond the railway at Westcroft Farm.

125. Residents moved into new houses on the L.C.C.'s Watling estate from 1927-31. Its charms were not immediately obvious to all residents, or neighbours, but as this c.1930 postcard shows the estate was well planned, with various house styles and retaining mature trees. Gardens, and community spirit, developed rapidly.

126. Led by Sir John Laing, the well-known builder, Christian Brethren opened Woodcroft Hall in 1928. They provided a Sunday school and, particularly until the Watling Centre opened in 1933, a place for community meetings.

127. Watling Avenue provided shops which also attracted non-residents, as this 1948 photo demonstrates.

128. Clitterhouse Farm photographed in 1926, shortly after an auction of its cattle and equipment had ended its history as a working farm. The fields north and east of the farmhouse were acquired by the U.D.C. in the same year and provided land for playing fields and for Hampstead Football Club. The club changed its name to Golders Green FC in 1933 and in 1946 took its present name of Hendon FC. The farmhouse and some of its outbuildings still survive. Clitterhouse School was built on the site immediately opposite in 1934.

129. Laing's Golders Green estate, centred on Pennine Drive, was built over part of Cricklewood Aerodrome. This had been opened by Handley Page in 1916 on fields from the southern part of Clitterhouse Farm and remained in use until 1930. The Clitterhouse playing fields are seen again on the bottom left of the picture.

130. This rural scene, with signposts pointing left to Finchley and Southgate and right to Hampstead and London, is the junction of the new Watford and Great North Ways at Fiveways Corner in 1927. Although Sunny Hill Fields can still be seen behind, this is now a fully urban roundabout with, since the late 1960s, the M1 flyover passing overhead.

131. Hendon Way near The Vale in 1935. Like the other new arterial roads of the 1920s it was soon lined with new houses, initially protected by the wide verges. Many services came to the new residents: the photo features a window cleaner's trolley and a laundry van.

132. Apex Corner, alias Northway Circus, was created in the mid-1920s at the junction of the new Watford and Edgware Ways (A1 and A41). The Apex garage can be seen at the back of this 1940s postcard.

133. The view along Golders Green Road towards the junction with the new North Circular in 1927. The Swiss Cottage and the neighbouring Chatterbox or Albert Row were demolished in 1933 and eventually replaced by Riverside Drive, a large block of luxury flats which were occupied by 1939. The wooden building is Suckling's Forge and the gate to its adjoining cottage can be seen at the edge of the picture. The cottage survived until 1992 when it was demolished and a large office block built on the site.

134. The old Mutton or Decoy Bridge was replaced when Bell Lane was widened in 1931. Decoy Farm, seen on its south-east, was an 18th-century building with some 20th-century mock Tudor timbering. It was demolished in 1935.

135. Brent Cross, the junction of Hendon Way and the North Circular, seen here *c*.1947, was built in the mid-1920s. A flyover opened in 1965. The junction was again altered as part of a wider scheme which included the construction of the adjacent shopping centre, which opened in 1976.

136. The Deansbrook, at this point the boundary between Hendon and Edgware, at the Splash in Hale Lane *c*.1925. Imminent change is evident: there is a Cross's estate agent's board in the field beyond, and the pipes for culverting lie next to the ford.

"I simply called"

The HOME SEEKERS
GUIDE TO

MILL HILL

For all particulars apply to

WILLIAM HOLLIS

Mill Hill Property Exchange
MILL HILL, N.W. 7.

137. William Hollis was established in 1879 and was one of the firms most actively engaged in developing Mill Hill, Hendon, Finchley and Angmering-on-Sea (West Sussex) in the 1920s. This brochure is typical of many produced to entice new residents to the area.

138. Dole Street was the connection from Sanders Lane to Milespit Hill, running between Ashley and Wise Lanes. Dislike of this ancient name, which seems to be a variant of Dollis, led to its suppression in the mid-1940s.

139. There was a forge in Mill Hill in 1685, but its location is unknown. In the 19th century there were three, including this one at the foot of Holcombe Hill where Charles Balaam was smith and farrier from at least 1821. It survived longer than most but closed in 1932, being replaced for another 20 years by the shop and tea rooms shown here.

140. This postcard of The Burroughs catches the *White Bear* shortly before it was rebuilt in 1931-2. The inn has a long history: it is probably one of the buildings shown on a 1597 map, and manor courts were frequently held there up to 1916.

141. After problems in the 1860s, Hendon created a sewage farm just below the Brent, near today's Brent Cross, from 1886. This photo, taken in 1930, records one of its final extensions since Hendon became part of the West Middlesex Drainage Scheme in 1931, and the farm was superseded by a new one at Mogden (Isleworth) in 1935.

142. Hendon opened its first library in The Burroughs in 1929, on the previously empty site between the town hall (1901) and fire station (1914) – also visible in this 1930s postcard. The library's imposing exterior was preserved during extensive internal remodelling in the early 1970s.

143. Grove House (or Hendon Grove), which stood just north of The Burroughs, was one of the largest houses in Hendon. It was built by 1753, but substantially altered in the 19th century when it became a private mental hospital. Its spacious grounds included the land on which the town hall, library and fire station were built. This photograph was taken in 1933, one year before the house was demolished. Part of the gardens have been retained as a small public park.

144. Mill Hill Fire Station in Hartley Avenue opened in 1929, and both it and the surrounding development were new when this picture was taken. Hendon U.D. was striving to provide the range of services its enlarged population required.

145. Hendon's first pool opened at The Hyde in 1922, three years before this picture was taken. A second pool, also open-air, opened at Daws Lane Mill Hill in 1935. Following the opening of Copthall Pools in 1977, both the earlier pools closed in 1980.

146. The Regal, Finchley Road has a fairly typical history. It opened as a skating rink in 1929-30 but was converted to a cinema in 1932. In the late 1950s it was converted again, to a bowling alley. When this too closed the building stayed empty until demolition and commercial replacement.

147. By the 1930s cinema was probably the most popular form of entertainment and no suburb was without its 'modern cathedral'. The Ambassador at Hendon Central was one of Hendon's most spectacular picture palaces. This photograph of its splendid art deco interior was taken before its grand opening in 1932. Typically, it has since had several changes of name and management and today survives as an MGM three-screen cinema, but sadly with a much altered interior.

148. This view up Church Road from The Quadrant was taken in 1952. The junction acquired three of its four imposing buildings, and its new name, in the 1920s. The Odeon, a serious rival to the Ambassador, opened on the fourth corner (earlier Cook's Corner, see plate 88) in 1939. The last Odeon to open before the Second World War, it survived until 1979, and has been replaced by housing.

149. Brent Bridge House, an 18th-century mansion in beautifully landscaped grounds along the Brent, became a highly successful hotel in 1918. This was the dining room *c.*1935, probably just before the first commercial television receiver in Britain was installed in it in 1936. The hotel closed in 1974 and was then demolished.

150. It was unfortunate that the Watford Way sliced through Mill Hill Park, created in 1924 from the fields of Daws Farm. One benefit, though, was the council's grant of a site on the west of the road for the London University Observatory. This opened in 1929, although the telescope shown here is older. Nearby, Will Hay the comedian, a serious astronomer, built an observatory in his garden at Great North Way, from which he discovered a spot on Saturn in 1933.

151. The first Jewish families began to move into the area following the opening of Golders Green station, but it was not until the 1920s that their numbers increased significantly. The first purpose-built synagogue opened in Dunstan Road, Golders Green in 1922. This photograph shows the interior of Hendon Synagogue, Raleigh Close, which opened in 1935 replacing an earlier building on Brent Street.

152. West Heath Court, North End Road was first occupied in 1936 and is one of the many blocks of service flats which appeared in the area during the 1930s. The prominent advertising board, typically, describes luxury mansion flats and makes much of modern conveniences such as refrigerators, central heating and shower baths.

153. Staples Corner, with Staples mattress works on the south-west, as it looked *c.*1937. The whole junction was radically altered in the early 1970s when a flyover was built, and the adjacent southern end of the M1 was also constructed.

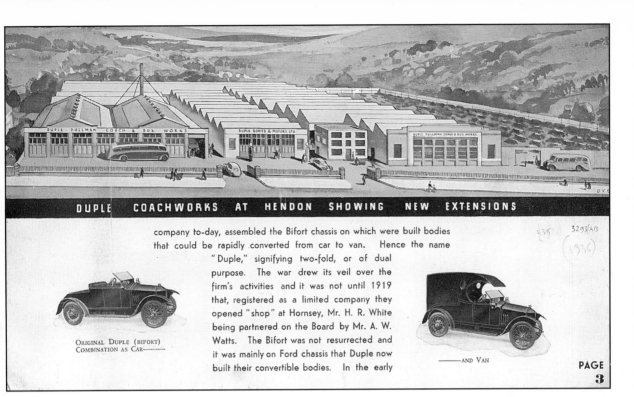

DUPLE COACHWORKS AT HENDON SHOWING NEW EXTENSIONS

company to-day, assembled the Bifort chassis on which were built bodies that could be rapidly converted from car to van. Hence the name "Duple," signifying two-fold, or of dual purpose. The war drew its veil over the firm's activities and it was not until 1919 that, registered as a limited company they opened "shop" at Hornsey, Mr. H. R. White being partnered on the Board by Mr. A. W. Watts. The Bifort was not resurrected and it was mainly on Ford chassis that Duple now built their convertible bodies. In the early

ORIGINAL DUPLE (BIFORT)
COMBINATION AS CAR——

——AND VAN

£35   3293/AB
(1936)

PAGE
3

154. Duple coachworks moved from Hornsey to The Hyde in 1925. The building of the factory had fallen so far behind schedule that the founder dismissed the builders and the work was completed by Duple employees. This brochure extract records the extensions which began in 1934 when the company purchased the adjoining Cowleaze Farm. Duple left the site in 1970 and it is now used by various light industrial concerns.

155. Hendon achieved borough status in 1932. Among the accompanying festivities was an ox-roasting, with the mayor in full regalia cutting the first portion. This is the scene as recorded in an Italian magazine, over the heading 'Bizzarrie inglesi'.

156. This imposing building on The Burroughs was originally the Hendon Technical Institute, built by Middlesex County Council in 1937-9. The photo was taken when it opened in September 1939, although the official ceremony was cancelled due to the outbreak of war. It was renamed Hendon Technical College in 1945, and Hendon Institute of Technology in 1962. In 1973 it became part of Middlesex Polytechnic, which in 1992 became Middlesex University.

157. A picture taken at the first 'Rout the Rumour' rally in England, held in Hendon Park on 21 July 1940. Organised by the Ministry of Information, it was intended to 'chase the chatterbugs and rout the rumour-mongers' and boost morale. Around 20,000 people attended and part of the rally, which featured performers such as Jack Warner, Will Fyfe and local resident Will Hay, was broadcast on the Forces' programme.

158. George VI and Queen Elizabeth, accompanied by Hendon's wartime mayor A. A. Naar, inspect the damage caused by a mine, which scored a direct hit on Colindale tube station on the night of 25 September 1940, causing several deaths and many injuries.

159. The Victoria British Restaurant on Brent Street, pictured in 1943, was one of several wartime civic restaurants opened in Hendon. Staffed by volunteers and managed by the council, their main purpose was to provide hot, nutritious midday meals for those employed in war work and unable to return home for lunch. A take-away service was also offered, although customers had to supply their own crockery. The restaurant site, on the corner of Victoria Road, is now occupied by Montcliff House, a block of offices.

160. The photograph records the devastation of the worst single bombing incident in Hendon, when a V2 rocket fell almost centrally over Ramsey, Ravenstone, York and Argyle Roads in West Hendon on the night of 13 February 1941. Eighty people died and 40 houses were totally destroyed with many others left in ruins. The picture was taken about two weeks after the incident, with removal vans and council trucks lining the streets, which have been cleared of rubble. The street pattern of this area changed completely after comprehensive redevelopment in the late 1960s.

161. The Medical Research Council bought land at Mill Hill in 1922, but permanent construction was slow to start and only the shell of the National Institute for Medical Research building was ready by 1940, when it was requisitioned and used for the duration of the war by the W.R.N.S. The scientists finally moved in 1949 and the Institute received its royal opening in 1950, the year of this photograph.

162. Seventeenth-century Church Farm, now a rare survivor from Hendon's rural past, was bought by the council in 1944. Two proposals for its demolition were defeated and instead it was restored and opened as a museum in 1955. Norman Brett-James, the well-known local historian, founder of Mill Hill Historical Society and major lobbyist for the museum, is seen here at the moment of ceremonially opening the door.

163. Church End Farm stood almost opposite Church Farm. The 19th-century farmhouse on the right replaced the older building seen behind the conservatory. This 1939 photo was taken from the roof of the Technical Institute which had just been built on some of the farm's lands, and whose expansion finally led to demolition of the farm complex in 1967. Only the gabled house on the left and adjacent milking parlour (just off the picture) of the Model Dairy Farm, built as part of Church End Farm in the 1870s, still survive. The name Church End Farm has, however, been transferred to one of the modern houses beyond the milking parlour.

164a & b. Hendon Council undertook large-scale housing redevelopment in several parts of the borough during the late 1950s to early 1960s. The first photo comes from a preliminary survey and shows North Street and New Brent Street in 1958. The second shows Granville Road at an intermediate stage in 1962.

165. Colindale Trolleybus Depot, originally a Metropolitan Electric Tramways' tram depot, was the site where the first prototype trolleybus in London was demonstrated in 1909. However, it was to be another 27 years before London Transport replaced trams with trolleybuses in Hendon. The photo shows one about to leave on Route 666 not long before they were scrapped in 1962. On the left of the picture, the old parish milestone marking the half-way point between London and Watford is clearly visible.

166. Main roads to the north, from Watling Street onwards, have often affected the area. This photograph from June 1965 shows roadworks for the new M1 at Station Road, Mill Hill.

The old forge, Mill Hill, by H. Norman, 1981